# Sustainability at the Cutting Edge

Emerging technologies for low
energy buildings

Peter F. Smith

Architectural Press

OXFORD   AMSTERDAM   BOSTON   LONDON   NEW YORK   PARIS
SAN DIEGO   SAN FRANCISCO   SINGAPORE   SYDNEY   TOKYO

Architectural Press
An imprint of Elsevier Science
Linacre House, Jordan Hill, Oxford OX2 8DP
200 Wheeler Road, Burlington MA 01803

First published 2003

**Disclaimer**   The information and statements herein are believed to be reliable, but are
not to be construed as a warranty or representation for which the author or publisher
assume legal responsibility. Users should undertake sufficient verification and testing
to determine the suitability for their own particular purpose of any information or
products referred to herein. No warranty of fitness for a particular purpose is made

**British Library Cataloguing in Publication Data**
A catalogue record for this book is available from the British Library

**Library of Congress Cataloguing in Publication Data**
A catalogue record for this book is available from the Library of Congress

ISBN 0 7506 5678 6

For information on all Architectural Press publications
visit our website at www.architecturalpress.com

Produced by Gray Publishing, Tunbridge Wells, Kent
Printed and bound in Great Britain by MPG Books Ltd, Bodmin, Cornwall

# Contents

# Acknowledgements

I am indebted to the researchers and construction professionals who readily gave permission for the inclusion of their illustrations in the text, in particular Dr Koen Steemers of Cambridge Architectural Research, Ove Arup and Partners, Whitby Bird and Partners, Christopher John Hancock for the image of Malmo, Jeremy Stacy Architects for the Council Offices, King's Lynn and Pilkington plc for the image of Herne Sodingen government training centre. I also owe my thanks to Dr Randall Thomas of Max Fordham and Partners and Robin Saunders of the Department of Mechanical Engineering, Sheffield University for reviewing the manuscript and giving me the benefit of their expertise in the sphere of renewable energy. I must also record my thanks to my wife Jeannette for her sterling work in making up for my deficiencies in proof reading. Finally my special thanks are due to Sir John Houghton who adapted his keynote conference address to be used as the opening chapter.

# Preface

In October 2001 the Royal Institute of British Architects (RIBA) hosted a conference on the subject *Sustainability at the Cutting Edge* which inspired the title of this book. The opening address was delivered by Sir John Houghton, a world authority on climate change issues. The aim of the conference was to provide an overview of the science and technology behind sources of renewable energy which would assume prominence in the next decade. This review was placed in the context of increasing concern about the impact of climate change and the fact that the built environment in countries like the UK is the worst culprit in terms of carbon dioxide emissions.

For a number of reasons global concerns about energy have reached a new pitch of intensity.

The attack on the World Trade Center of the 11 September 2001 was indirectly seen as a threat to the security of oil supplies especially from the Gulf states. In many states nuclear power plants are being decommissioned and most will not be replaced. In addition, there will be growing pressure to reduce carbon dioxide emissions under the Kyoto treaty.

Uncertainties regarding oil in terms of reserves, access and price are increasing. As the Princeton Professor and petroleum geologist Kenneth Deffeyes put it recently: 'we have ten years to get over our dependency on crude oil'.

Diminishing gas reserves are causing countries like the UK to be reliant on distant and sometimes unstable countries ultimately for up to 90% of supplies.

In the UK the competition is between nuclear and renewables, and on present performance the government is right to be sceptical about the capacity of renewables to fill the energy gap. For example, in terms of wind energy the UK had an installed capacity of 474 MW at the end of 2001 despite having the best wind resources in Europe. Germany, much less windy, had 8754 MW and even Spain could boast 3337 MW. The German target of installing photovoltaics in 100,000 homes by 2003 is well on the way to being achieved. Where is the UK in comparison? It is reckoned that wind and biomass together could provide the UK with 55–70% of total electricity needs by 2020.

However, all that was before the 11 September since which date sustainability has taken on a new meaning. Now we are faced with recalibrating our scales of vulnerability, especially in terms of the reliability of supplies of energy. As buildings are the largest single sectoral users of energy, this has particular concern for all involved in the construction industry.

In the situation that now prevails there is an opportunity for governments to adopt an energy policy covering the next 50 years leading ultimately to zero carbon dioxide emissions and which is risk free.

This is not an impossible dream. For example, the UK has probably the best range of natural resources in Europe from which to extract enough renewable energy to meet all its needs. What is required is for both the Treasury and the Department of Trade and Industry to be reprogrammed to think holistically and in a multi-modal context, which brings us to the technology.

Buildings have the potential to play a major role in a future energy scenario. They can be daytime power stations through photovoltaic cells (PVs) on roofs and elevations. At the moment PVs are not cost-effective set against conventional fossil generation. But things should now be different. Not only should we factor-in the climate change benefit but also the security gain. Quantify these and offset them against the cost and PVs become a bargain.

Soon we should see the next generation of PVs on the market, probably based on titanium which will be significantly cheaper than silicon-based cells, especially as a huge deposit of titanium has just been found in Australia. Already in Germany and Japan economies of scale are being realized, thanks to government support. By, say, 2020, here millions of homes and offices could be pocket power stations feeding the grid or creating hydrogen for fuel cells.

That's where the other major breakthrough will occur. Many analysts believe that fuel cells will be the prime energy source in the future both for buildings and transport. Their fuel is hydrogen and oxygen from the air and their product, water and electricity. Being modular they can be scaled to meet almost any requirement, from an individual home to a grid connected power plant. For the next two decades or so static fuel cells will get their hydrogen from reformed natural gas. By 2050 experts predict we will have fully embraced the hydrogen economy. Making hydrogen will be the principle energy related industry. Mark this quote from the President of Texaco Technology Ventures:

> *Market forces, greenery, and innovation are shaping the future of our industry and propelling us inexorably towards hydrogen energy. Those who don't pursue it, will rue it. (From an address to the US House of Representatives Science Committee)*

The sceptics will counter all this with the point that PVs, wind, etc. are intermittent sources of supply. How can you guarantee continuity from renewables? In technical terms, where is the base load coming from?

Two zero carbon renewable energy sources that are reliable and predictable are the tides and coastal currents. The UK has toyed with tidal power since the 1920s. Now there are technologies available which make tidal estuaries and coastal currents ideal candidates for the production of reliable electricity.

Wind energy will also be a major resource. The European Union has set a goal of 40 GW of installed capacity by 2010. That would produce 80 TWh of electricity and save 72 million tonnes of carbon dioxide. The industry has a target of 60 GW. For this to be possible ideal sites like the UK will have to pull their weight. At the moment, according to the European Union, existing framework conditions and other barriers are holding us back, a 'eurospeak' euphemism for planners. Perhaps foot-and-mouth disease will come to our rescue. Vast tracts of land have been vacated creating opportunities for farmers to diversify into power generation. A combination of tide, wind, biomass and PV coupled with significant reductions in demand would enable the UK henceforth to be self-sufficient in clean energy.

It was announced in October 2001 that thousands of American homes will soon receive their electricity through superconducting cables, cooled at their core by liquid nitrogen. The importance of this is that these cables offer virtually no resistance so there is no line loss. Normal transmission cables suffer around 10% line loss. At the same time, the importance for renewables is that superconductivity offers for the first time the prospect of high capacity electricity storage in superconducting coils. Energy can be drawn off from storage sub-stations as and when needed.

Alongside these supply initiatives it is essential that we look seriously at demand-side reductions. There is no excuse now not to embrace super-insulation standards for domestic buildings. It's time we abandoned our superstitious attachment to cavity walls. On the continent they have no problem with this.

In commercial buildings the main energy cost is often electricity, mostly for lighting. This is set to change dramatically with the development of light-emitting diodes (LEDs) producing white light. An LED around 1–2 cm will emit the equivalent of a 60 W bulb using only 3 W. It will have a life expectancy of 100,000 hours.

Developments in optical fibre technology will also transform the energy demand in the commercial sector. The photonic revolution is almost upon us, and will be fully realized when the barriers to photonic switching are overcome. Then the all-photonic computer will use much less power and generate almost no heat.

There is no doubt that information technology will progress at an exponential rate. Photonic materials will spearhead this revolution, Quite soon the whole world could be linked to an optical fibre superhighway based on photonic materials.

It is appropriate for a book of this nature that Sir John Houghton should set the tone.

# 1  Introduction

*The following is an edited version of the opening address to the 'Sustainability at the Cutting Edge' conference, RIBA, October 2001 by Sir John Houghton CBE, FRS. Co-chairman of the Scientific Committee of the UN Intergovernmental Panel on Climate Change.*

My theme is the problem of climate change and sustainability. In September 2001 the Intergovernmental Panel on Climate Change (IPCC) met in London to agree the final part of its third assessment report (TAR) (*Climate Change 2001*). Over 100 governments were present with their delegates, including governments such as Saudi Arabia who were there in force to try to weaken anything we could say. On the other hand some of the European states wanted to strengthen things beyond what was reasonable. So, we had a good mix of people, with 40 or 50 leading scientists representing the world science community. We worked for 10 days, morning, noon and night to agree a 20-page document. As a result the IPCC's latest report is very comprehensive in the way it considers the whole problem of climate change and its links to sustainability.

Figure 1.1 shows the flow of information and the flow of action within the climate change problem. It starts with emissions and changes in atmospheric concentrations of carbon dioxide and other greenhouse gases produced from industrial and other sources. These result in changes of climate that impact on human activities and ecological systems in a number of ways. Action will be necessary to adapt to these changes, which in some places will be large. There are actions also which can be taken to mitigate the emissions and so reduce the impact.

There are three parts to the IPCC 2001 report covering first, the science, secondly the impacts and adaptation and thirdly the options for mitigation. Summaries of these three parts can be found in the Synthesis Report which is the final part of the TAR and which addresses nine policy questions. The complete report is on the IPCC website (www.ipcc.ch).

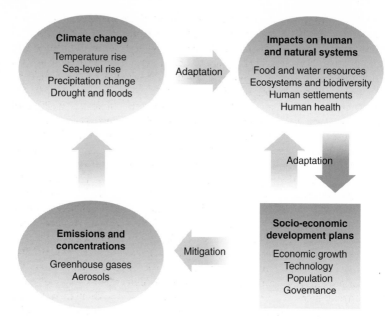

**Figure 1.1**   Flow of information and flow of action within the climate change problem.

## The science of climate change

So what is global warming about? Claude Monet loved the London of 100 years ago because of the smog and the light percolating through it. London still is quite polluted – I live in west Wales and when I come to London I notice the difference in the atmosphere. We could clean it up much faster and much more efficiently than we are doing, but there has been progress. That is *local* pollution.

During the past 15 or 20 years, we have learned about a new form of pollution namely, *global pollution*. By global pollution I mean pollution for which I am responsible that actually affects the whole world. The first example of this concerned ozone in the stratosphere. Very small quantities of chemicals containing chlorine emitted into the atmosphere caused ozone to be depleted in a catalytic way – a major problem of global pollution. The problem of climate change arises in a similar way. The carbon dioxide I emit, or cause to be emitted, from my home, industry, motorcar or airplane lives in the atmosphere for at least a hundred years and affects the climate through an increase in the greenhouse effect. Because of its effect on the climate it is affecting everybody in the world.

You all know how the greenhouse effect works – solar radiation comes in and warms the surface of the earth largely unimpeded by the atmosphere *en route.* Infra-red radiation is emitted outwards from the surface but is partially blocked by 'greenhouses gases' such as water vapour, carbon dioxide and methane which re-emit it back to earth. This 'greenhouse' shield acts as a blanket keeping the planet substantially warmer than it would otherwise be. In fact, if it were not for these gases, the surface would be at a temperature of around −15°C, instead of around +15°C on average. The 'natural' greenhouse effect is therefore responsible for 20–30°C of warming; and without it the whole earth would be covered by ice.

As the amount of carbon dioxide in the atmosphere increases because of emissions from human activities, the greenhouse effect increases and the earth's surface becomes warmer. How do we know this warming is occurring? If we look at temperature records over the last millennium in the northern hemisphere, periods can be identified like the little ice-age or the medieval warm period but the changes in average temperature over the whole hemisphere were small – of the order of a few tenths of a degree until the nineteenth century. However, since the start of the twentieth century the temperature over the whole globe has risen considerably well over half of a degree on average. In particular, since the 1970s it has risen more sharply – a rise that we believe is almost certainly due to the influence of increased greenhouse gases such as carbon dioxide, methane, etc. Other factors have also contributed to this warming such as solar variations and volcanic eruptions. But the dominant factor over the past 50 years has certainly been the increase in greenhouse gases, and by far the dominant factor in the future will be their continuing increase in use.

Since the industrial revolution the level of carbon dioxide has gone up by over 30%. Methane, another important greenhouse gas, has doubled over that period due to factors connected with humans, such as cattle rearing, leakage from landfill sites and from oil and gas wells. To put the carbon dioxide increase in the perspective of a longer timescale, say 160,000 years, we can ascertain the atmospheric composition in the past from the analysis of pockets of air trapped in ice cores drilled several kilometres to the very bottom of the ice in Antarctica or Greenland (Figure 1.2). Temperatures over these millennia can also be ascertained from the ratio of the isotopes of oxygen in the ice that provides an indication of the temperature at which the ice was laid down.

You will see that there were variations in both temperature and carbon dioxide during the last ice age that tracked each other very well – providing support for the influence of carbon dioxide on the temperature. The carbon dioxide concentration now in the atmosphere is around 350 parts per million by volume (ppm). The likely carbon dioxide concentration at the end of this century will be 600 or 700 ppm if we continue with business as usual. This takes it way beyond anything it has been for many millions of years – a very large change indeed in one of the factors that controls the earth's climate. Regarding the ice ages, we know that they are triggered by variations in the earth's orbit round the sun. These variations are based on astronomical data that can be determined accurately. The next ice age is due

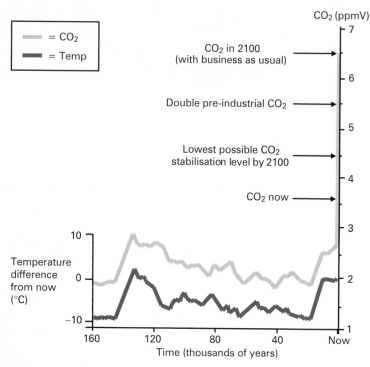

**Figure 1.2**   The last 160,000 years (from ice cores).

in about 50,000 years; anything we do now is not likely to impact much on what is going to happen then.

Figure 1.3 shows a comparison between observations and models of the global average temperature over the twentieth century. Climate models are like meteorological forecasting models but much more elaborate. In fact they are the most sophisticated models that have yet been generated of any physical system. By including variations in the various forcing factors on the climate such as variations in the sun, in volcanic activity and the greenhouse gases, you will see that modelled variations in the twentieth century temperature compare reasonably well with observations. Then, using models to project temperature changes into the future, an increase of somewhere between 2 and 5°C is expected in the twenty-first century – the range representing uncertainty in just what the profiles of emissions of carbon dioxide and other greenhouse gases will be and also uncertainties in the actual model projections.

An increase of, say, 3°C in global average temperature doesn't sound very much. I suspect that the temperature in this lecture theatre has gone up by something like that since we all walked into it half an hour ago. But remember that this is a global average temperature – that is an average over the

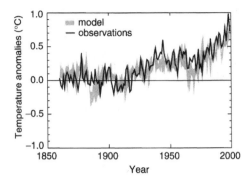

**Figure 1.3** Simulated annual global mean surface temperatures. (From IPCC Synthesis Report 2001.)

whole world – and that the difference between the middle of an ice age and the warm periods in between ice ages is of the order of 5 or 6°C in terms of global average temperature. So a 3°C change in global average temperature is half an ice age in terms of climate change and we are talking of that happening not over many thousands of years as has occurred in ice ages, but over a hundred years or so during this century. That will be the most rapid rate of climate change that the earth has experienced, certainly for 10,000 years and probably for a lot longer.

It is the rapid rate of change that is the main problem because it will be very hard for humans to adapt, and also for eco-systems to adapt especially in our very crowded world where the possibilities for humans to move or migrate is severely restricted.

## The impacts of global warming

Talking about global average temperature is, however, not very helpful; we need to know what it means in terms of impact? That we are increasingly vulnerable to the likely impacts of climate change has been realized during recent decades, for instance, by insurance companies. Before the 1980s the insurance companies thought there was no storm that could cause more than a billion dollars of damage leading to insurance claims. Now there are storms regularly that cause $20 billion or $30 billion of insured damage. If you happen to be a name at Lloyds, you will know what I am talking about. A big part of the increase is because more people are insuring and also because more people are living in coastal areas or other vulnerable places. But the insurance companies need no convincing that there is also an element of climate change behind the escalating claims.

The first important impact concerns sea level rise The earth warms up and the oceans warm and expand. The main reason for sea level rise is expansion of ocean water. In addition, glaciers have been melting for many decades and now quite rapidly. The ice caps will grow a bit in the middle because of increased snowfall and they will tend to melt round the edges. The net effect on the ice caps is probably small at the moment. However, if the temperature rises more than a few degrees, Greenland will start to melt down, although complete melt-down will take several millennia.

The likely rise of sea level this century is, on average, about half a metre – which will have a big impact. It will, for instance, affect your business as architects because of the impact on buildings since many buildings are close to the coast. Nevertheless, on the whole, in countries like our own, or even the Netherlands, we can cope with it – although at significant cost.

However, in a country like Bangladesh, where there are tens of millions of people living a metre below sea level, not only is there sea level rise due to global warming but the ground is sinking for other reasons too. Building adequate sea defences around Bangladesh and many other such delta areas is just not feasible. Further, the delta region is good agricultural land so inevitably people are compelled to live there to survive. Where else can they go?

This is just one illustration of the many people at risk world-wide because of sea level rise – many people live near the coast in many parts of the world.

Regarding sea level rise, I should also point out that the lower levels of the ocean will take many centuries to warm so sea level will continue to rise at about half a metre per century for many centuries. With several kilometres of ocean depth to warm we are talking of rising sea levels for a long time to come.

Another major impact will be on water supplies. There is much more demand for water around the world and it is becoming an increasingly scarce resource. Water is often shared between nations (e.g. the Nile and the Jordan) and Boutros Boutros-Ghali, the last Secretary-General of the United Nations, has suggested that the next war will be about water rather than about oil – he is probably right.

Computer models of the climate provide indications of the impact on the hydrological cycle if the amount of atmospheric carbon dioxide were doubled – a probable scenario. A warmer world is a wetter world because there is more evaporation. There is also more energy in the atmospheric circulation. This is because the main energy of the circulation comes from the release of latent heat from water vapour as it condenses. As the amount of water vapour increases, so does the amount of latent heat released and the intensity of the circulation. The result is a more vigorous hydrological cycle with more heavy rainfall events.

But, interestingly also, these models tend to show that not only will wet areas tend to become wetter but also that some semi-arid regions will tend to become drier The reason for this is that with a more intense circulation, rising air will tend to reach higher levels where it is both colder and drier. Consequently, it is likely that there will be less rainfall in some dry regions. A general message is, therefore, that global warming will tend to lead to more floods and more droughts. Now, floods and droughts are the biggest disasters that the world knows. On average they cause more economic damage, more misery and deaths than any other disaster. Their likely increasing frequency and intensity is not good news.

To provide some impression of what these impacts will mean, there is a telling statistic compiled by Norman Myers at Oxford of the number of refugees by 2050 that might be caused due to sea level rise and because of floods and droughts and other problems associated with global warming. It is a careful and conservative study and comes up with an estimate of the likely number of refugees of 150 million. That of course is small compared with the world's population but it is half the population of the United States! We live in a crowded world where refugees on that scale would create large problems. The world could be facing not only a problem of global warming, but also a problem of global security.

So much for impacts, except to say that not all impacts will be negative, a few will be positive impacts and some people will be better off. Northern Europe will probably be able to grow more food. Northern Canada and Siberia will be warmer with a longer growing season. In these very northern places, provided your house is not built on the permafrost in which case it will probably have to be rebuilt, you will probably be better off. So there will be winners as well as losers but because adjustment to change will tend to be difficult and expensive – and sometimes even impossible – there will be far more losers than winners.

## What is being done about climate change?

I mentioned at the beginning what scientists have been doing, through the IPCC. It is a remarkable story; the world's scientific community has got together to write reports with a consensus about them which I think is almost unique in science, certainly in a subject which is so uncertain in much of its detail.

Politicians also got together in 1992 at the Earth Summit in Rio when they all signed, including the first President Bush for the United States, the Framework Convention on Climate Change (FCCC) which states an ultimate objective to achieve stabilization of greenhouse gas concentrations at a level which would prevent 'dangerous anthropogenic interference with the climate system' and which would also allow for sustainable development. It is a remarkable statement and the conference of the parties to the FCCC has been working since then on the appropriate action to be taken. The Kyoto Protocol was formulated and given broad agreement in 1997. That Protocol is an important first step. It is the first time that nations have got together to agree, with one or two notable exceptions, something which is essentially binding and which will not only oblige them to cut down emissions but also provide an opportunity to trade emissions between nations – people love trading! It has still to be ratified by enough nations; this hopefully will occur by the end of 2002.

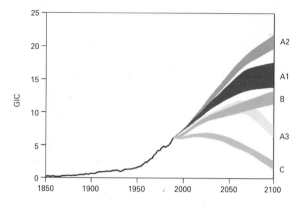

**Figure 1.4**  Global carbon emissions from fossil fuel. (From IIASA/WEC Global Energy Perspective 1998.)

What sort of action is required? Global emissions of carbon dioxide at the moment due to the burning of fossil fuels amount to about 6 or 7 gigatonnes of carbon per year. Business as usual will take those emissions to 15 or 20 billion tonnes by the end of this century unless something is done about it. The curves on the right of Figure 1.4 come from the World Energy Council (WEC) – the body that speaks for the world's energy industries. The lowest line is the only one that stabilizes carbon dioxide concentrations as required by the climate convention. The WEC report says that it would be possible for the world to follow the line provided everyone really tried hard with renewable energy and energy efficiency.

It is not just the problem of us in the developed world reducing emissions, there are developing countries that wish to increase their emissions because they want to industrialize. A great disparity exists in emissions between the rich and the poor nations – that is a big problem and international action is required to address it. The principles that need to underlie such action are the Precautionary Principle, the Polluter Pays Principle (e.g. through measures such as carbon taxes or capping and trading arrangements), the Principle of Sustainable Development and lastly a Principle of Equity across the nations and across the generations.

Figure 1.5 comes from the Global Commons Institute – the proposal it describes is called contraction and convergence. It shows emissions of carbon dioxide in the past, in the present and predictions for the next 100 years, the sources of emissions being divided into major country groupings. The overall envelope is an emissions profile that would stabilize carbon dioxide concentrations in the atmosphere at 450 ppm, not dissimilar to the curve in Fig. 1.4. It peaks within a few decades from now and then comes rocketing down to well below today's value of emissions by the end of the century. An emissions profile stabilizing at 550 ppm has a similar shape but at somewhat higher levels.

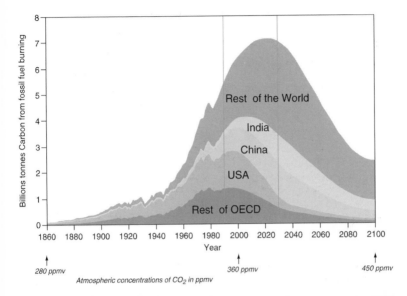

**Figure 1.5** Carbon dioxide contraction for 450 ppmv and convergence by 2030 to globally equal per capita emission rights. (From the Global Commons Institute.)

How can the burden of emissions reductions be shared equitably between nations? The Global Commons Institute argues that the only fair way to share it out is to give every person in the world the same allocation of carbon dioxide emissions. That is shown in the diagram as applying from the year 2030; between now and 2030 is the period of 'convergence'. That is a very radical proposal; for instance the allocation to someone in the UK would be less than 20% of our current average per capita emissions. The only way it could be achieved would be through carbon trading between nations. Industrialized nations would buy carbon credits from countries in the developing world, where the per capita rate of carbon emissions is below the target average so that the carbon gap progressively narrows ultimately to zero. This proposal well illustrates the problem and the type and scale of action that is necessary; it is also one that meets to a good degree the four principles we mentioned above.

How are the reductions in emissions going to be achieved? There are many possibilities and the technology that is necessary for increasing energy efficiency and for reducing fossil fuel use is largely available. First, consider buildings which are responsible for about one-third of total emissions worldwide. According to the IPCC report, a reduction of emissions from buildings by about 60% could be achieved by using much more efficient devices and appliances, insulation, better design and control, etc.

Let me emphasize the importance of integrated design. The tradition in building whereby the design of various components and services are pursued in isolation, can be highly inefficient particularly in energy use – but also in terms of cost. Much could be achieved by changes in working practices as described by people like Amory Lovins from the Rocky Mountain Institute in Boulder, Colorado. He has proposed a factor-four principle: energy use could easily be cut by a factor of four or more at less overall cost and with a more user-friendly overall design.

Renewable energy has enormous potential. It just needs to be developed as quickly and effectively as possible. That means more research and development and more effective government support. In the UK we are lagging behind countries like Germany or Japan where renewable energy sources are being brought on-line and the gains through economies of scale being realized substantially more quickly. We have the potential to do it, we can make money from it. In the UK it is not being exploited on anything like the scale which is required.

Just to summarize, global warming is a significant problem. The impacts will cause damage this century amounting to a few percent in the growth of gross national product (GNP), much more in developing countries than developed countries. There is action we can take. Technology is available. What is the cost of that action? Some actions we can easily take will actually save money. Overall, the best economic studies show that by 2050 or so the reduction in the growth of GNP might be some fraction of one per cent. Greater innovation may bring the cost even lower. And climate change links with many other issues, environmental and otherwise, in this whole story of sustainability and the pursuit of quality of life.

Many leading industrialists and politicians have picked up the issue and are putting out good messages. Two leading oil companies, BP and Shell, have embraced the challenge. The prime minister has very recently been talking about a range of world problems that need attention, solving not just global warming, but also other global problems such as that of poverty. As Sir Crispin Tickell has said, a major problem is that 'we know what to do but lack the will to do it'. We need to acknowledge that this is a moral and spiritual problem. We need to address moral and spiritual goals as well as economic objectives within our society.

So, you say, what can I do about it, I'm just me? A good 200 years ago the British parliamentarian Edmund Burke said 'no-one made a greater mistake than he who did nothing because he could only do a little'. We have got to begin to treat our earth much more responsibly and to recognize it is much more fragile than we realize.

# 2 Solar thermal power

It is likely that solar thermal power will provide a major share of the renewable energy needed in the future, since solar radiation is by far the largest potential renewable resource. About 1% of the earth's deserts covered with solar thermal plants would have supplied the world's total energy demand for the year 2000.

The solar thermal resource serves two energy domains: heat and electricity.

## Solar heating

The United Nations Development Programme (UNDP) world energy assessment estimates the global use of energy to heat water to be 10,000 PJ. This technology is especially important for rapidly growing cities like Mexico City and São Paulo which have a severe pollution as well as an energy problem.

There are two basic systems for solar heating:

- flat bed collectors
- vacuum tube collectors.

Flat bed collectors consist of metal plates coated matt black behind glass or plastic. They are tilted to maximize uptake of solar radiation. Behind the plates are pipes carrying the heat absorbing medium, either water or air. Water for indirect systems contains antifreeze. The underside of the plates is insulated. Flat-bed collectors realize temperatures around 35°C and are best employed to supply pre-heated water for a gas boiler or immersion heater.

It is increasingly becoming the case that the collector system incorporates a photovoltaic (PV) module to provide power for the circulating fan, making it a true zero fossil energy option.

### Vacuum tube collectors

In this technology evacuated tubes enclosed within an insulated steel casing work by exploiting the vacuum around the collector. This reduces the heat loss from the system making them particularly suited to cooler climates like that experienced in northern Europe. They heat water to around 60°C but sometimes significantly higher. This means that domestic hot water systems may have no need of additional heating. To realize their full potential they should be linked to a storage facility which stores excess warmth in summer to supplement winter heating (see Fig. 2.1).

Solar panels have traditionally been associated with providing domestic hot water. Solar water heaters comprise a solar collector array, and energy transfer system and a thermal storage unit. There are two basic principles involved:

- passive or thermosyphon systems in which circulation of the working fluid is driven by thermal buoyancy
- active solar whereby a heat transfer fluid is mechanically circulated through the collector.

There is a further division into direct or 'open loop' systems in which potable water is circulated through the collectors and 'closed loop' or indirect systems which use an antifreeze heat transfer circulating fluid.

**Figure 2.1**   Vacuum tube solar collectors on Professor Tony Marmont's Farm, Nottinghamshire.

**Figure 2.2** Thermosyphon flat plate collector with direct connection to horizontal tank. (Courtesy of *Renewable Energy World*, March–April 2002.)

In thermosyphon systems the storage tank must be above the collectors. There are three configurations which can be directly connected to a horizontal tank:

- flat bed collectors
- parabolic trough collectors with the heat pipe absorber (see below) feeding directly into the base of the storage cylinder
- evacuated tube collectors.

This combined collector/storage system is limited to providing hot water during the day (see Figs 2.2–2.4).

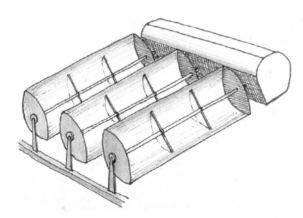

**Figure 2.3** Parabolic trough collectors (SunTrack) with heat pipe absorber inserted directly into horizontal storage tank.

**Figure 2.4** Thermosyphon evacuated tube collectors with connection to header storage tank. (Courtesy of *Renewable Energy World*.)

Active systems can be open loop (Fig. 2.5) or closed loop in which the circulating fluid passes through a coil heat exchanger within the storage tank (Fig. 2.6).

The technology is being promoted by the International Energy Agency (IEA) via its Solar Heating and Cooling Programme. The IEA is an agency of the Organization for Economic Co-operation and Development (OECD). The potential for solar domestic hot water is about 1 m$^2$ of collector area per person.

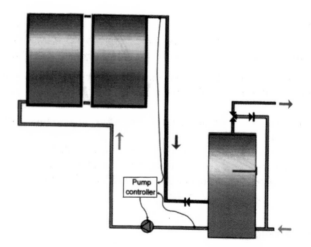

**Figure 2.5** Open loop pumped circulation system. (Courtesy of *Renewable Energy World*.)

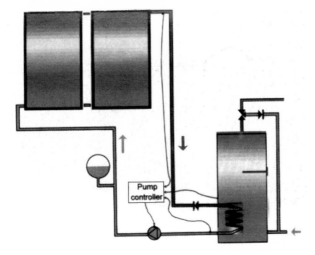

**Figure 2.6**  Closed loop (indirect) pumped circulation system with internal coil heat exchanger. (Courtesy of *Renewable Energy World*.)

Countries like China and those in the Middle East are exploiting this technology at an accelerating pace with 10 million m² already installed in China and yearly sales of 3 million m². The market in China is five times larger than that in Europe. In 2001 China produced 20 million all-glass evacuated tube collectors. World-wide, the installed area is about 30 million m².

## Economics

While this technology is one of the cheapest renewable options, it is still not cost effective weighed against fossil-based energy with a payback time of around 20 years. The market will only grow significantly at this stage if:

- there is direct or indirect government support for the technology
- following this intervention, the market expands to achieve economies of scale
- the product is of the highest quality and fitting procedures simplified and standardized
- there is an adequate network of trained and accredited specialist installers
- complete roof modules incorporating solar collectors are made available to the construction industry for new build, making the marginal cost of the collectors relatively moderate.

### Solar buildings

Solar collectors are one of several renewable technologies that together make a solar building. It is essential that, from the earliest design stage, there is a symbiotic relationship between active solar and PVs, heat pumps and possibly small-scale wind turbines. 'Integrated design' is one of the slogans of the new millennium.

Well-designed solar houses can reduce energy demand by a factor of four against conventional homes. This has been demonstrated by the IEA Solar Heating Advanced Low Energy Buildings. With the addition of PV, it is possible for buildings to become net energy producers.

The effectiveness of solar thermal applied to the existing housing stock is slightly reduced. Nevertheless, many buildings produced in northern Europe in the 1950–60s are seriously in need of renovation. If solar technology is absorbed into the overall cost and economies of scale are realized the payback time should be considerably less than the normal 20-year timescale.

In the UK there is an acute problem of poor-quality housing, much of it dating from the nineteenth century, which is associated with fuel poverty, ill health and substantial unnecessary winter deaths.

In the case of commercial buildings, cooling and lighting often outweigh the heating as the dominating energy sink. This aspect of energy efficiency has been considered in some detail elsewhere.[1]

In Europe there are wide variations in the application of active solar heating. For example, Austria has almost 18 m$^2$ per 1000 inhabitants of installed capacity compared with the UK that boasts about 0.2 m$^2$. Yet the UK climate is not all that different from that of Austria.

### Solar–gas combination boilers

The principle here is that a 240-litre tank is heated by flat plate solar collectors supplemented by a gas burner within the body of the cylinder. It provides space heating and domestic hot water. A heat exchanger coil in the upper half of the tank heats the central heating circuit. A production solar–gas combination boiler with 2.83 m$^2$ of solar collector produces 4 GJ/year; a 5.4 m$^2$ collector supplies 5.64 GJ/year. A test involving 25 units showed a boiler efficiency of 90.1%. On average, consumers saved 650 m$^3$ of natural gas compared with their former systems. Based on the present price of gas (1999) the payback time is 13 years. However, gas prices are rising. The other factor to consider is that the system would be almost zero carbon if at some future date it employed biogas (see Fig. 2.7).

### Active district solar heating

Flat plate or evacuated tube solar heating collectors are a well-established technology for individual buildings, especially at the domestic scale. The next development is likely to be the scaling up of this technology to help meet heating requirements at district level. According to Dirk Mangold of the University of Stuttgart:

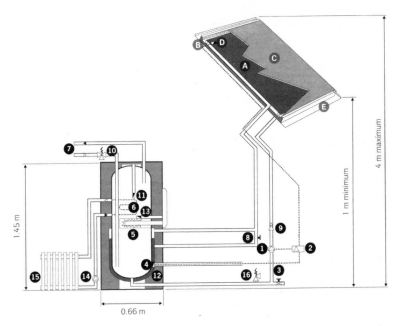

**Figure 2.7** Solar-gas combination boiler. 1. Pump. 2. Delta temperature control. 3. Supply tap. 4. Temperature sensor in the boiler. 5. Gas burner. 6. Central heating coil. 7. Hot and cold water pipes. 8. Level tap. 9. Maximum flow restrictor. 10. Intake combination. 11. Thermostat control for boiler. 12. Boiler insulation material – CFC-free. 13. Outside temperature control. 14. Central heating pump. 15 Radiator. 16 Maximum pressure valve. A. Absorber. B. 40 mm insulation plate – CFC-free. C. Low-iron tempered glass. D. Temperature sensor in the collector. E. Aluminium rim. (Courtesy of Caddet.)

*Central solar heating plants offer one of the most economic ways of providing thermal solar energy to housing estates for domestic hot water and room heating. Over 50% of the fossil-fuel demand of an ordinary district heating plant can be replaced by solar energy when seasonal heat storage is included in the plant.*[2]

District solar heating plants consist of a network of solar collectors that may be sited on ground-level rigs next to a central heating substation. In urban situations it is more likely that solar collectors will be mounted on roofs. In Germany and Sweden complete solar roof modules are available for construction purposes, complete with rafters and insulation. The flat-plate collectors replace the tiles. Compared with a conventional roof the additional cost is between €150–250/m² of flat-plate area including all pipe work and installation cost.

There are two basic systems of district solar heating: seasonal storage and diurnal storage.

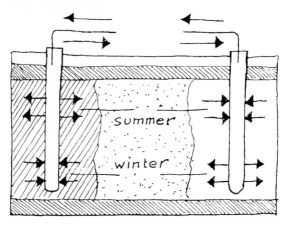

**Figure 2.8**   Aquifer heat storage.

## Central solar heating plants for seasonal storage (CHSPSS)[3]

Banking heat in summer to meet winter expenditure is the principle behind seasonal storage. There are four principal storage technologies.

### Aquifer heat storage

Naturally occurring aquifers are charged with heat via wells during the warming season. In winter the system goes into reverse and the warmth is distributed through the district network (see Fig. 2.8).

### Gravel–water heat storage

A pit with a watertight plastic liner is filled with a gravel–water mix as the storage medium. The storage container is insulated at the sides and top, and base for small installations. Heat is fed into and drawn out of the storage tank both directly and indirectly (see Fig. 2.9a).

### Hot-water storage

This comprises a steel or concrete insulated tank built partly or wholly into the ground (see Fig. 2.9b).

### Duct heat storage

Heat is stored in water saturated soil. U-pipes are placed in vertical bore holes which are insulated near the surface. Heat is fed into and out of the ground via the U-pipes. Storage temperature can reach 85°C (see Fig. 2.9c).

Central solar plants with seasons storage aim at a solar fraction of at least 50% of the total heat demand for space heating and domestic hot water for a housing estate of at least 100 apartments. The solar fraction is that part of the total annual energy demand which is met by solar energy.

(a)

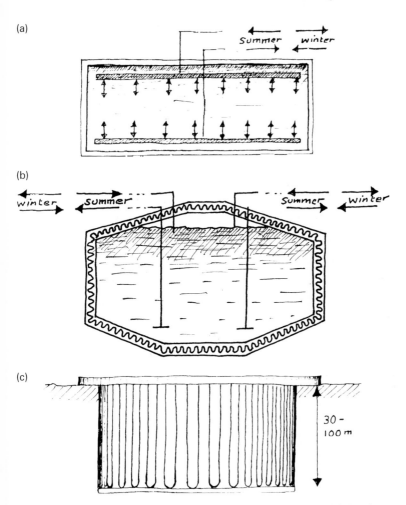

**Figure 2.9** (a) Gravel–water heat storage; (b) hot-water storage; (c) duct heat storage.

In all these installations it is necessary to receive authorization from the relevant water authority.

At the time of writing, Europe has 45 MW of installed thermal power from solar collector areas of over 500 m². The ten largest installations in Europe are in Denmark, Sweden, Germany and the Netherlands mostly serving housing complexes. Germany's first solar-assisted district heating projects launched as part of a government research project 'Solarthermie 2000' were at Ravensburg and Neckarsulm. These have already proved valuable test beds for subsequent schemes.

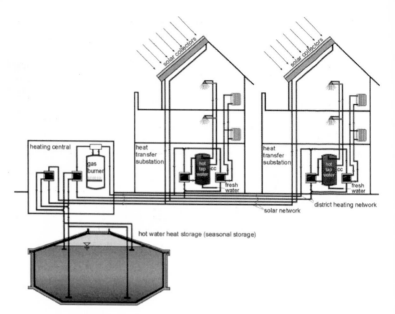

**Figure 2.10**   Diagram of CSHPSS system, Friedrichshafen. (Courtesy of *Renewable Energy World*.)

One of the largest projects is at Friedrichshafen which can serve to illustrate the system (see Fig. 2.10). The heat from 5600 m$^2$ of solar collectors on the roofs of eight housing blocks containing 570 apartments is transported to a central heating unit or sub-station. It is then distributed to the apartments as required. The heated living area amounts to 39,500 m$^2$.

**Figure 2.11**   Seasonal storage tank under construction, Friedrichshafen. (Courtesy of *Renewable Energy World*.)

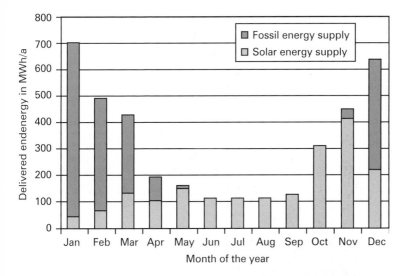

**Figure 2.12** Monthly ratio of solar to fossil-based energy at Friedrichshafen. (Courtesy of *Renewable Energy World*.)

Surplus summer heat is directed to the seasonal heat store which, in this case, is of the hot water variety capable of storing 12,000 m$^3$. The scale of this storage facility is indicated in Fig. 2.11.

The heat delivery of the system amounts to 1915 MWh/year and the solar fraction is 47%. The month-by-month ratio between solar- and fossil-based energy indicates that from April to November inclusive, solar energy accounts for almost total demand being principally domestic hot water (see Fig. 2.12).

The Neckarsulm project is smaller, serving six multi-family homes, a school and a commercial centre amounting to a heating area of 20,000 m$^2$. The roof-mounted solar collector area comes to 27,000 m$^2$ to satisfy a heat demand of 1663 MWh/year. In this instance the solar fraction is 50%. The storage facility is a duct heat storage tank with a capacity of 20,000 m$^3$ (see Fig. 2.13).

### Central solar heating plant diurnal storage (CSHPDS)

In this case, the storage capacity is obviously much less, merely coping with a 24-hour demand. The demonstration project at Ravensburg supplies 29 terraced houses with hot water and space heating via a four-pipe district heating network. It is calculated that this should meet 11% of the total heat requirement of the estate (see Fig. 2.14).

Solar systems with diurnal storage are mainly used to supply domestic hot water to large housing estates, large apartment blocks or hostels. They are designed to achieve a solar fraction of 80–100% in summer, representing 40–50% of annual heating demand in central and northern Europe.

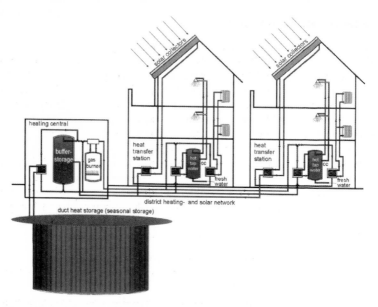

**Figure 2.13**   Diagram of the Neckarsulm project. (Courtesy of *Renewable Energy World*.)

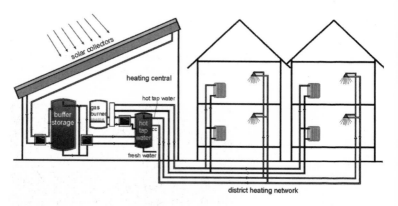

**Figure 2.14**   Diagram of the Ravensburg central solar heating plant diurnal storage project. (Courtesy of *Renewable Energy World*.)

Both seasonal and diurnal systems should be designed as part of a comprehensive energy efficiency programme involving insulation and rational energy conversion and supply. This can result in energy savings of 60% against the current norm.

## Solar thermal electricity

Solar energy is more evenly distributed across the sun belt of the planet than either wind or biomass. The downside is that deserts do not attract centres of population. However, as the world gradually switches to becoming a hydrogen-based energy economy, solar thermal electricity could be the key to substantial hydrogen production by electrolysis. African countries bordering the Mediterranean could greatly boost their economies by exporting solar hydrogen to Europe by tanker or pipeline. This may also be the future for the Gulf states. (see Chapter 12).

In response to a challenge by the European Union in 1999, the Soltherm Europe Initiative was launched. Its aim is to install 15 million $m^2$ of thermal solar collectors in Europe by 2004. The European Commission's White Paper 'Energy for the Future' set a target of 100 million $m^2$ across Europe by 2010.

There are four key elements to solar thermal power technologies:

- *concentrator* – that captures and focuses solar radiation
- *receiver* – this absorbs the concentrated sunlight transferring the heat energy to a working fluid
- *transporter-storage* – that passes the fluid from the receiver to the power conversion system; in some systems a proportion of the thermal energy is stored for later use such as night-time
- *power conversion* – this is the generation phase via a heat engine such as a stirling engine or steam engine.

There are two basic types of concentrator:

- *Parabolic trough collector.* This system comprises long parallel rows of concentrator modules using trough-shaped mirrors. It tracks the sun from east to west by rotating on a linear axis. The trough collector focuses

**Figure 2.15**   Solar thermal parabolic trough collector. (Courtesy of Caddet.)

**Figure 2.16**   Parabolic dish solar concentrator in Australia. (Courtesy of Caddet.)

sunlight onto an absorber pipe located along the focal line of the trough. A heat transfer fluid, typically oil heated to 400°C or water to 520°C is transported through the pipes to drive a conventional steam power generator (see Fig. 2.15).

- *Solar central receiver or 'power tower'*. In this instance an array of mirrors or 'heliostats' is arranged around a central axis, focusing solar radiation onto the focal point of the array. A receiver situated on a tower at the focal point transfers the solar heat to a power block in the form of a steam generator (Fig. 2.16).

Research is being conducted into ultra-high energy towers which can heat pressurized air to over 1000°C then to be fed into the gas turbines of combined cycle systems.

**Figure 2.17**   Parabolic Sundish with Stirling engine the 'Powertower' in the USA. (Courtesy of *Renewable Energy World*.)

A version produced in the United States by STM Power of Michigan links their 'SunDish' tower system to a Stirling engine to produce electricity (see Fig. 2.17).

A criticism of solar thermal plants is that they are only effective in daytime. The Australian National University has met this challenge head-on by developing a sun dish which focuses radiation onto a thermochemical reactor containing ammonia. Under the intense heat the ammonia is broken down into hydrogen and nitrogen which is then stored at ambient temperature. It is stored in lengths of former natural gas pipelines. When needed the gases are recombined using an adapted industrial ammonia synthesis reactor. The 500°C of heat generated by the recombination is used to generate steam for a conventional power plant. The beauty of the system is that the gases are constantly recirculated within a closed loop. The leaders of the research team, Dr Keith Lovegrove and Dr Andreas Luzzi, claim that a solar field the size of a suburb would power a city the size of Canberra.

A major advantage of solar thermal systems is that they can be integrated into existing conventional power technologies. This will ease the transition to a fully renewable electricity supply system in the long-term future. In large measure this will be achieved by the re-powering of existing fossil-fuel plants.

There is confidence in the industry that future developments of this technology will deliver much higher efficiencies while driving down costs of electricity to a level that will compare favourably with conventional power plants.

## Solar thermal: the future

Solar thermal is still suffering from the problem that it has emerged out of the plumbing sector of industry resulting in certain mind sets which inhibit innovation. The following are some pointers to the way ahead.

### Modular design

Solar heaters must become an off-the-shelf item, with standardized connectors and in modules based on the amount of hot water required by one person.

### Simplified design

The installation procedures should be foolproof, making wrong connections inherently impossible. For example, many manufacturers still do not offer a standardized sleeve at the top end of the absorber to enable a sensor to be correctly inserted. Design rationalization would not only speed up installation time and reduce costs but also bring solar panels into the do-it-yourself market.

### Legionella

This is a waterborne bacterium that multiplies at between 40 and 50°C which is the average temperature of water storage including solar. It is potentially fatal if inhaled, for instance when showering. In some countries regulations require a minimum storage temperature of 70°C to be achieved at least once a day. This is the blanket bombing technique which has a negative impact on the efficiency of the collectors due to scaling problems which arise at over 60°C.

There are other possibly more effective ways of killing the bacteria. Ultraviolet light at high intensity destroys the bacteria's ability to reproduce and is frequently used for water purification. It is still not used in solar thermal systems. Used in combination with ultrasonic waves or anodic oxidation it should remove the source of problems like biofilms in the pipes. This would be more efficient than achieving a high temperature for part of a day.

### Antifreeze

It is standard practice to include an antifreeze agent in the collector for obvious reasons. The antifreeze agents are toxic, expensive, have a poor ability to carry heat and can change viscosity which can cause leaks. To avoid the need for antifreeze, some systems automatically drain-off when there is not enough solar gain. Another approach would be to design an absorber which can accommodate the expansion accompanying freezing. It could be that the time taken to melt the ice as the sun rises would be compensated for by the higher efficiency of a system without antifreeze.

### Storage

It was stated earlier that storage tanks should be insulated. There is still insufficient importance attached to this aspect of the system. Just as vacuum tube collectors are now available, so the next logical step is to have vacuum storage tanks which would maximize heat retention.

### Solar control units

There is still some way to go to make these user-friendly. They tend to be difficult to handle and are expensive for the function they perform, which is often merely to control a pump's on–off position. Often faults in a system are not discovered until an excessive heating bill arrives from the utility. Pressure, temperature and flow rates could easily be displayed in a living room with a red light indicating a fault.

### Intelligent systems

We are in the age when computers can learn by feedback. Intelligent systems could learn about consumers' behaviour and adjust heat output accordingly. For example, it would be possible to adjust the collector pump to reduce its rate of flow in order to increase the water temperature to coincide with the regular time occupants take a shower. It may only require 20 litres at enhanced temperature to meet this need. Over time an intelligent system will learn to finely tune supply to demand, thereby minimizing the involvement of a back-up heater.

Improvements are often avoided by being hit with the argument of cost-effectiveness. This can be an excuse for avoiding changing designs and manufacturing techniques. In the case of solar thermal, simplified and standardized installation procedures should considerably reduce the 21% of total system cost currently spent on installation. Add to this the fact that the system is more efficient and faults detected instantly, then the added costs should easily be offset, bringing them overall close to the heat production costs of conventional energy sources.

A major cost burden is imposed by the use of copper for piping. The high cost of copper is unlikely to change. In fact it is a commodity likely to rise as demand increases, ironically driven partly by the growing popularity of renewables. Plastic pipes are becoming more common. New materials such as reinforced silicon hose which is gas-tight and which can cope with high temperatures and offers a degree of expansion will be a suitable alternative. It is flexible which means that installation procedures are simplified. Add some clever connectors which can be installed on site and materials like silicon will capture the market.

Finally, the manufacture of solar thermal devices needs to make the transition from small-scale labour-intensive entrepreneur operations to high-output industrial mass production using specialized component manufacturers. This will not only change the image of the technology, but would also cope with its predicted rapid growth as the energy infrastructure becomes increasingly stressed due to geopolitical factors and problems of security of supply.

For the information on the future I am indebted to Cornelius Suchy, renewable energy specialist with MVV Consultants and Engineers, GmbH.

## Notes

1. Smith PF. *Architecture in a Climate of Change.* Oxford: Architectural Press, 2001.
2. *Renewable Energy World*, May–June 2001.
3. The data in this section were drawn from a paper by Dirk Mangold in *Renewable Energy World*, May–June, 2001.

# 3   Low energy techniques for cooling

The cooling of buildings is one of the largest of all energy sinks and therefore a major contributor to carbon dioxide emissions. This chapter considers a range of alternatives which fall into two categories:

- technologies which involve an external or stand-alone source of energy
- systems which are integrated into the structure and fabric of a building.

## Ground coupling using air

In the UK the ground temperature below 2 m is fairly constant, ranging between 10 and 14°C. Ideally the soil temperature should be 12°C or less. This makes it a suitable source of cooling in summer and possibly warmth in winter. The system operates by passing air through a network of pipes set at 2–5 m below ground. The soil temperature is roughly the same as the average yearly ambient temperature.

Best results are obtained when the circuit of pipes is positioned within gravel or sand and below the water table.

A number of factors influence the design of such a system:

- actual soil temperature
- velocity of the air through the pipes
- diameter of the pipes
- extent of the underground network
- conductivity of the soil
- moisture level of the soil.

The cooled air can be used directly as a cooling agent or it can provide pre-cooled air for conventional ventilation or air-conditioning.

In the context of this technology it is necessary to check for ground pollution, especially radon gas (see Fig. 3.1).

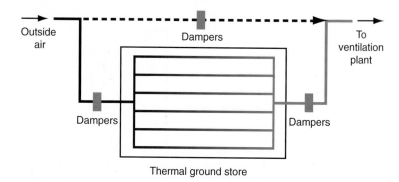

**Figure 3.1**   Ground source air cooling. (Courtesy of Building Research Establishment (BRE).)

## Ground water/aquifer cooling and warming

Alternatives to full air-conditioning with chillers that make heavy demands on electricity and fossil fuel for space heating are coming increasingly into prominence. One option is aquifer thermal energy storage. (AETS). This uses water from an underground well to cool either a building or an industrial process. Once the water has taken up the heat from the building, it can be returned to a second warm well and used to preheat ventilation air in winter.

Two boreholes are drilled to a depth of between 30 and 150 m. The wells should be between 100 and 150 m apart.

Where there is no movement of ground water ATES uses layers of water for cold and heat storage. In summer cool ground water passes through a heat exchanger where it cools the water system of the building which, in turn, cools incoming air in an air-handling unit.

The ground water, having absorbed the building's heat, is injected into the warm well. During the winter the system is put into reverse.

It is estimated that ATES can achieve from 60–80% energy savings compared with conventional air-conditioning. It has quite a short payback time to recover the additional investment of 2–8 years (see Fig. 3.2).

In situations where there is ground water movement the system can be used as a heat source or sink for a heat pump (see below).

In the UK the extraction and use of ground water is subject to approval by the Environment Agency.

### Evaporative cooling

Evaporative cooling is a relatively old technology that is being resurrected. This technique exploits the principle that molecules of a substance in a vapour state contain much more energy than the same molecules in a liquid state. The amount of heat needed to change a substance like water into

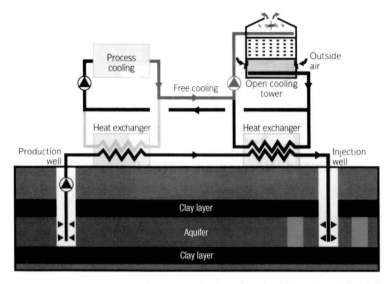

**Figure 3.2**   Aquifer cold water/warm water storage system. (Courtesy of Caddet.)

a vapour is its latent heat of evaporation. The heat is removed from the liquid and transferred to the vapour, causing cooling of surfaces in the process. This is the cooling system employed by nature in humans to lower the body temperature through perspiration.[1]

Direct evaporative cooling is achieved when incoming air is blown directly across a wetted medium or through a water spray. In this instance evaporative cooling provides 'sensible' cooling, i.e. experienced by the senses, while increasing the latent heat content of the air. The process is called 'adiabatic cooling' where the sensible heat removed from the air equals the latent heat absorbed by the water evaporated as the heat of vaporization.

This method of cooling can be created by intelligent landscaping, as when incoming air first passes over the surface of an external mass of water. An example where this technique is to be seen is at the University of Nottingham. In its Jubilee Campus the prevailing winds cross an artificial lake before being directed into the building by an inclined plane of glazing.[2]

Indirect evaporative cooling occurs when exhaust air is cooled using evaporative techniques and then used to cool the incoming air by being passed through a heat exchanger.

One of the most ambitious uses of evaporative cooling is to be found in the atrium of the Federal Courthouse of Phoenix, Arizona, USA designed by Richard Meier. The environmental engineers, Ove Arup & Partners, were challenged by the fact that the external temperature could exceed 40°C in summer which undermined the normal stack effect, so much a feature of atrium design in Europe. At the same time the air is dry, with a relative humidity level of around 40%. This made the building an ideal candidate for evaporative cooling. The design predictions were that the atrium temperature would be no greater than 30°C for 60% of the year and an additional 3°C for a further 15% of the year. This was deemed acceptable for a transition space between the extreme heat of the outside and the air-conditioned environment of the court rooms.

The evaporative strategy was to locate water sprays at the top of the atrium which serve to create a curtain of cooled air between the atrium and the adjacent balconies. The air then escapes at low level (see Fig. 3.3).

The Malta Stock Exchange offers an interesting variation on the theme of evaporative cooling. The interest lies in the fact that it is an existing chapel converted to this new function. Being a historic building, its walls have high thermal mass. The architect chosen was Brian Ford of WSP Environmental and formerly of Short Ford & Partners who designed the celebrated Queen's Engineering building at Leicester's de Montfort University. He opted for a passive downdraught evaporative cooling (PDEC) solution. The major advantage of PDEC is that it is driven by buoyancy dynamics alone, removing the need for mechanical assistance.

A raised roof ridge accommodates the misting jets and cooling pipes. Fresh air is drawn through centre pivot vents in the side of the ridge which is then cooled by evaporation. This sets up a downdraught cooling the atrium below. In summer automatic high level vents allow the night-time air entering at low level to pre-cool the building.

In the event that internal relative humidity level is above 65% the evaporation nozzles are automatically switched off and chilled water is directed to the cooling pipes. This causes cool air to descend into the atrium, while the warm air rises up the sides of the atrium to be cooled and then descend. Energy has to be used to chill the water but there are no fans which typically use 30% of the energy of an air-conditioning system. There is also no ductwork or air handling units.

Thermal modelling predictions indicated that electricity savings of 50% would be realized against a conventional air-conditioning system (see Fig. 3.4).

Air-handling systems that involve the warming of water carry a theoretical risk of legionella. Evaporative cooling can create pre-cooling of

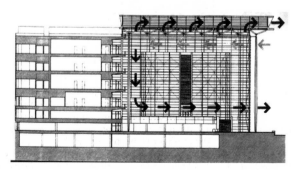

**Figure 3.3**  Evaporative cooling, Phoenix Courthouse.

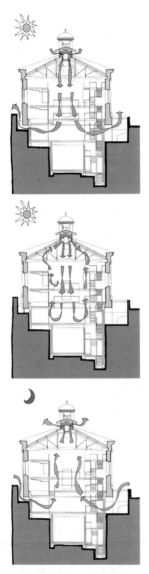

**Figure 3.4**  Sections and ventilation paths, Malta Stock Exchange.Courtesy of WSP Environmental. *Top*: Summer cooling to the atrium is provided by a combination of passive evaporation, cooling coils and night-time cooling. When outside temperature is high and relative humidity below 60% misting nozzles operate and cooling air is drawn through side vents in the ridge; *centre*: above relative humidity of 65%, nozzles switch off and chilled water in the cooling pipes takes over the cooling function; *bottom*: at night ridge vents opened and cool air is drawn from low level, rising by stack effect to exit at high level, pre-cooling the structure in the process.

ambient air for dry air coolers. This lowers the temperature of the water in the system which reduces the risk of this disease compared to a wet cooling tower.

Advantages of evaporative cooling include:

- the fact that it can be combined with conventional systems
- the heat exchanger in indirect systems can be used for heat recovery in winter if the exchanger is located within the exhaust air pathway.

## Phase change cooling

A phase change material (PCM) is one which changes its state from solid to liquid when subjected to heating and vice versa when cooled. Water is the obvious example. When it changes from a solid (ice) to a liquid it absorbs large amounts of heat before it shows any increase in temperature. A PCM which changes its state at temperatures around the range for thermal comfort is ideal for moderating temperature in buildings. One such material is sodium sulphate and its variant Glauber's salts which is a decahydrate of sodium sulphate. Glauber was a German chemist born in 1604, yet another case of an early discovery waiting centuries to find its true 'vocation'. It changes from a solid to a liquid at around 28°C, absorbing large amounts of heat and thus cooling the air in its vicinity. The reverse operation creates heat when the PCM returns to the solid.

A variation on the theme of phase change cooling has been produced by researchers at Nottingham University's Institute of Building Technology. The underlying principle still uses a chemical heat sink to soak up the heat in the air and pump cool air into a building. It is a highly energy efficient system, using only a fraction of the energy consumed by conventional air-conditioning. It is a system particularly suited to temperate climes where a few degrees of cooling can achieve comfort temperature.

The system invented by David Etheridge and David Rae draws daytime warm external air by fan over an array of fluid-filled heat pipes. The pipes conduct heat to storage modules containing a solid PCM. The PCMs located in the ceiling void absorb the heat as they slowly melt during the day, providing cool ventilation air (see Fig. 3.5).

During the night the opposite occurs. Shutters to the outside air are opened and the fan reverses direction to draw the cool air over the PCMs causing the material to solidify. The heat generated in the process is dumped outside the building (see Fig. 3.6).

The whole operation works on the principle that latent heat is stored in the PCMs. Their temperature hardly changes throughout the cycle since it is their latent heat capacity which brings about the change in air temperature.

The system is capable of being fine tuned to suit specific circumstances by adding chemicals which change the melting point of the PCM.

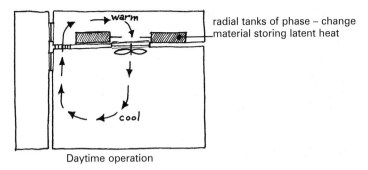

radial tanks of phase – change material storing latent heat

Daytime operation

**Figure 3.5** Phase change cooling. Fan draws warm air from the room which passes over phase change tanks cooling in the process as PCM changes from solid to liquid.

The researchers claim that this method of cooling is more agreeable to the occupants than conventional air-conditioning which often produces zones of excessive cooling while, at the same time, excluding the possibility of receiving natural ventilation via open windows. The Nottingham system is not affected by being supplemented by additional natural ventilation.

Perhaps the greatest virtue of the system in the context of the Kyoto Protocol is that its energy costs are merely one sixteenth those of conventional air-conditioning with obvious carbon dioxide emission benefits.

## Daytime operation

Another system for solar cooling is being developed in the Nottingham laboratories. Evacuated tube solar collectors heat water to around 110°C. The resultant high-pressure steam is expelled at around mach 2. The steam passes through an ejector where the Venturi effect causes the pressure to drop. A liquid refrigerant is fed to the ejector where it vaporizes under the vacuum

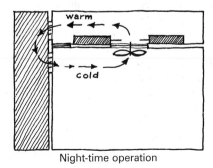

Night-time operation

**Figure 3.6** Phase change cooling. At night the fan reverses direction and the external vents open. Cool air is drawn over the PCM which cools and solidifies.

created in the ejector causing a cooling effect which is transmitted to the internal space. This adiabatic cooling drops the temperature to −1°C. The low pressure steam exiting the ejector is condensed and the water recirculated. In the Nottingham project the evacuated heat pipe array collects 13 kW of solar heat and converts it to 6 kW of refrigeration. The system is backed up by natural gas when the temperature is high but cloudy conditions cut out the solar gain. This system is patented but not yet licensed.

## Desiccant dehumidification and evaporative cooling

In some environments a combination of high temperature and high humidity defies a remedy by conventional air-conditioning which is biased towards temperature rather than humidity. Dehumidification is merely a by-product of bringing the temperature down to below the dew point of the air causing condensation.

A desiccant is a hygroscopic material, liquid or solid, which can extract moisture from humid air, gas or liquids. Liquid desiccants work by absorption where moisture is taken up by chemical action. Solid desiccants have a large internal area capable of absorbing significant quantities of water by capillary action. Examples of efficient desiccants are:

- silica gel
- activated alumina
- lithium salts
- triethylene glycol.

This method of dehumidification requires a heating stage in the process. This is to dry or regenerate the desiccant material and requires a temperature range of 60–90°C. One option is to supply the heat by means of evacuated tube solar collectors, backed up by natural gas when insolation is inadequate. Alternatively waste heat, for example from a Stirling combined heat and power (CHP) unit, may be exploited.

As a full alternative to air-conditioning, desiccant dehumidification can be used in conjunction with evaporative cooling. After being dried by the revolving desiccant wheel the air passes through a heat exchanger such as a thermal wheel for cooling. If necessary, further cooling may be achieved by an evaporative cooler before the air is supplied to the building.

The exhaust air at room temperature also passes through an evaporative cooler and then through the thermal wheel, chilling it in the process. This enables the thermal wheel to cool the supply air. After passing through the thermal wheel the air is heated and directed through the desiccant wheel to remove moisture and then expelled to the atmosphere.

There are problems with the system. It is not amenable to precise temperature and humidity control and it is not so efficient in dry climates. On the positive side it is providing a full fresh air system (see Fig. 3.7).[3]

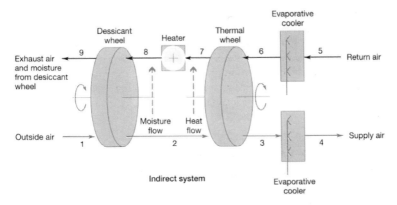

**Figure 3.7** Desiccant wheel and thermal wheel dehumidifying and cooling.

## Solar-assisted desiccant dehumidification with air-conditioning

In certain extreme environments it is necessary to couple desiccant dehumidification with conventional air-conditioning. However, the pre-conditioning of the air reduces the load on the air-conditioning plant.

As in the case above, the system has two air pathways, incoming and outgoing. The incoming path draws external air through a slowly revolving desiccant wheel that draws off the moisture and delivers the dried air to the air-conditioner. In the other path, hot air from the building is further heated by evacuated-tube solar collectors serving a heat exchanger to regenerate the desiccant material in the revolving wheel before being ejected from the building.

This system is especially appropriate for restaurants and kitchens which can experience extremes of both temperature and humidity (see Fig. 3.8).[3]

A further advantage of this system is that it can remove pollutants from the air. It also has the benefit of being able to offer a continual supply of fresh air, unlike full air-conditioning.

## Refrigeration

The inventor of refrigeration technology was Albert Einstein better known for solving the riddle of the universe. This innovation was responsible for the explosion in the sale of domestic refrigerators which occurred in the 1930s. The compressor refrigerator is based on a thermodynamic cycle whereby a gas is compressed mechanically causing it to heat up. After discharging its heat, the gas, still under pressure, liquefies. The liquid is allowed to expand by lowering the pressure. In the process it evaporates, absorbing heat from its surroundings. The relationship between the cooling capacity and the power needed to achieve it is called the coefficient of

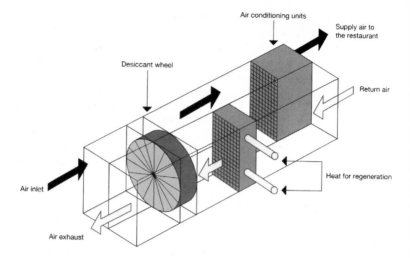

**Figure 3.8**   Desiccant wheel dehumidifying and cooling system (Courtesy of Caddet *Renewable Energy Newsletter*, March 2000.)

performance (CoP). For well-designed machines this can approach 100%. In a solar-linked system, PVs could provide electricity for the compressor.

## Ammonia-absorption cooling

In the case of ammonia-absorption cooling the operation relies on the fact that ammonia is soluble in cold water but not in hot water. When a solution of water and ammonia is heated ammonia vapour is driven off at high pressure.

If this gas is then cooled in a condenser to ambient temperature it becomes a liquid. This pure liquid ammonia is brought into contact with a small amount of hydrogen gas in an evaporator. This causes the ammonia to revert again to a gas, absorbing heat from its surroundings in the process. This is the cooling phase of the process.

The ammonia–hydrogen mix is then brought into contact with water at the absorber at ambient temperature. At this temperature the ammonia is able to dissolve into the water leaving the pure hydrogen to be returned to the evaporator for the process to begin again.

There is no mechanical support for the circulation process which is driven by a 'bubble pump'. This comprises a narrow vertical heated vessel where bubbles form, lifting the liquid in the process. The most common application of bubble pump technology is the *espresso* coffee machine. This pump is cheap and maintenance free.

The technology has some inherent problems such as the fact that if the boiler does not reach a critical temperature it does not drive off all the ammonia as a vapour which, in turn, undermines the effectiveness of the purification of the hydrogen. As the evaporation temperature of the ammonia in the evaporator depends on the vapour pressure of the ammonia in the hydrogen, an inadequate boiler temperature would significantly reduce the cooling efficiency of the system.

The basic system requires the boiler which heats the ammonia–water mix to reach a temperature of 150°C. In solar energy terms this can only be achieved by solar concentrators. Researchers in the Technical University of Vienna redesigned the cycle inserting an additional loop called a 'bypass' which makes it possible to extract much more ammonia from the ammonia–water solution at a relatively lower temperature than was previously possible. As a result, a boiler temperature of 75–80°C brings about the necessary evaporation of ammonia. This brings the technology within the range of normal evacuated tube solar collectors for providing the heat. This is the ideal heat source since it is at its most abundant during the summer when cooling is in greatest demand.

To provide space cooling a fan drives ambient air over the evaporator to be ducted from there throughout the building.

The heat source could also be spare heat from a CHP system driven by an internal combustion engine, a micro-turbine or a Stirling engine (see Fig. 3.9).

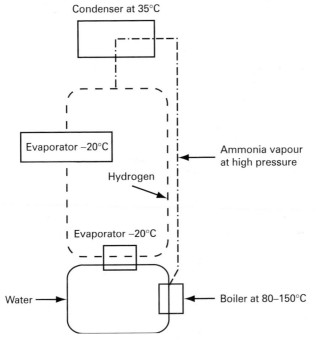

**Figure 3.9**   Ammonia-absorption cooling system.

## Thermionic cooling

It was in 1883 that Thomas Edison discovered this phenomenon, but it was not until 1994 that Gerald Mahan published a rather pessimistic paper on the prospects for this form of refrigeration. It is based on an electrical device called a vacuum diode which goes under the name of the Cool Chip. It contains two thin films separated by a narrow vacuum layer. If a voltage is put across the gap the most energetic electrons on the negative side 'boil off' carrying their kinetic energy to the positive side of the chip. As the hottest electrons migrate, the negative side or cathode cools, opening up the prospect of chemical-free refrigeration. The additional energy in the electrons reaching the positive anode is merely dissipated as heat. This is the basis of thermionics.

A British company called Borealis is optimistic that this technology has considerable potential, offering 80% efficiency as against the 30–50% of a compressor refrigerator. A panel of 25 chips covering 5 cm$^2$ would operate a typical domestic refrigerator using about 15 W of electricity. It has the advantage of being silent, with no moving parts, and therefore virtually maintenance free. It remains to be seen if the technology can be scaled up to provide cooling for buildings. Indirectly it has the potential for reducing the cooling load in buildings by cooling microprocessors and other electrical equipment that make a significant contribution to the heat build-up in offices.[4]

## Night-time cooling

At the start of the chapter it was stated that there is a category of cooling which uses the building fabric as a component of the system. The most elementary is night-time cooling.

### With natural ventilation

This method makes use of the exposed thermal mass of a building to be cooled by the outside air during the night. Exposed concrete floors are the most effective cooling medium. Vaulted or coffered soffits offer the maximum radiant surface. The cooling stored in the fabric is released as radiant cooling or an air stream directed over surfaces during the day. Vents or windows are automatically opened at night to admit the cool air. During the day, warm air is vented to the atmosphere. The fact that it is radiant cooling may allow the air temperature to be slightly higher than the norm while still maintaining comfort conditions.

Night cooling of a high thermal mass structure can offset about 20–30 W/m$^2$ of heat gain during the day, reducing the peak temperature by about 2–3°C.

The system is optimized if there is cross-ventilation and internal solar gains are kept to a minimum. The method works best if there is a large diurnal temperature range with night temperature below 20°C. Also, the best results are achieved in narrow open plan spaces, say 15 m maximum between façades. There is the limitation that heat gains should not exceed 30 W/m².

### With mechanical ventilation

In this case the cooling potential of night-time air is optimized by being forced through the building fabric by fans. At the same time it assists in expelling warm air during the day. The system has the advantage that it eliminates the need to have open windows either day or night. It also offers control over the supply and extract air flow.

A variation is described as the 'enhanced surface heat transfer system'. A perforated metal sheet is applied to the underside of the floor slab leaving an air gap. Air is mechanically forced into the gap creating turbulent air currents which appreciably improves the heat transfer between the air and the slab maximizing night-time cooling. The external air can be ducted directly to the gap or emitted into the room and then recirculated through the ceiling gap. As with natural ventilation the night-time temperature should be below 20°C. However, the heat gains that can be accommodated can increase to 50 W/m² (see Fig. 3.10).

## Hollow core slab

Precast concrete floors with integral connected ducts can effectively move either cool or warm air throughout a building. The air is in contact with the thermal capacity of the concrete before entering the occupied space. This

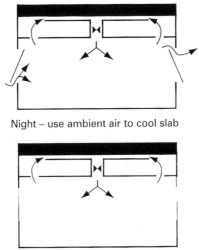

Night – use ambient air to cool slab

Day – cooled slab reduces air temperature

**Figure 3.10**   Enhanced surface heat transfer system. (Courtesy of BRE.)

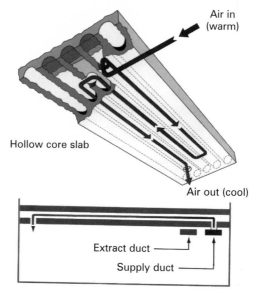

**Figure 3.11**  Hollow slab natural ventilation. (Courtesy of BRE.)

is a highly efficient means of achieving a high rate of air-to-slab heat transfer and vice versa and therefore the charging and discharging of cooling.
The soffit of the slab should be exposed to effect maximum heat exchange
with the occupied area. In this condition the hollow core slab can offset heat
gains by up to 50 W/m². One of the best-known proprietary systems using
this technique is Termodeck from Sweden (see Fig. 3.11). There will be a
further reference to this system in Chapter 15.

## Chilled beams and ceiling

Water is the heat transfer medium in this technology circulating at the relatively high temperature of 16°C. Chilled beams create convective air movement to cool a room. In chilled ceilings a flat soffit panel provides radiant
and convective cooling.

Chilled beams can provide about 60 W/m² of cooling water at 16°C and
a room temperature of 26°C.

Chilled ceilings provide roughly 40 W/m² assuming 50% active area;
otherwise as for chilled beams.

## Notes

1.  Thomas R ed. *Environmental Design*, pp. 12–13. London: E & FN Spon, 1996.
2.  Smith PF. *Architecture in a Climate of Change*, pp. 127–128. Oxford:
    Architectural Press, 2001.
3.  *Caddet Renewable Energy Newsletter*, April 1995.
4.  *New Scientist.* 'Boiling fridges' pp. 30–31, 24 January 1998.

# 4 Geothermal energy

Heat contained within the planet causes macro-geological events like earthquakes, volcanoes and tectonic movement. Geothermal energy in the context of this book refers to that small fraction of the earth's heat which can be converted to useful energy. Most of this heat is generated by decaying radioactive isotopes within the earth's mantle.

The rate of increase of temperature according to depth in the ground is called the 'geothermal gradient' and averages 2.5–3.0°C per 100 m of depth. Modern drilling techniques can penetrate up to 10 km.

Where there are active geothermal areas this gradient can increase by a factor of ten producing temperatures above 300°C at 500–1000 m. This occurs where there is an upward intrusion of high temperature rocks from the magma belt. In such circumstances a temperature of around 600°C can be expected at depths from 5 to 10 kms. This would provide high pressure steam. However, useful geothermal energy is available at the normal geothermal gradient.

This heat has to be brought to the surface. Geothermal springs do this spontaneously. More often, water has to be injected into the hot, permeable rocks known as the 'thermal reservoir', where it circulates absorbing heat in the process. If there are several geothermal wells in a vicinity, this is described as a 'thermal field' (see Fig. 4.1).

An advantage of geothermal energy is that it is independent of climate or seasonal/diurnal variation. The capacity factor of geothermal plants is often in excess of 90%, producing energy at a price which is lower than most other renewable technologies.

## Geothermal electricity

According to one authority, geothermal represents 42% of the electricity produced by the combination of wind, solar, tidal and geothermal. Electricity

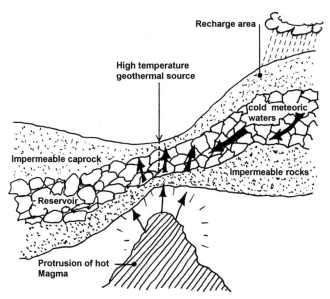

**Figure 4.1** Schematic diagram of the geothermal system.

generation mainly involves conventional steam turbines which operate at a minimum of 150°C. There are two principle types of steam turbine that are described below.

### Atmospheric exhaust turbine

This is a relatively straightforward technology which is economical to install. Its output usually ranges from between 2.5 and 5 MWe.

### Condensing turbines

This technology has more auxiliary equipment than atmospheric exhaust plants and is much larger with output reaching 100 MWe. It is more expensive *pro rata* due to its complexity, but, by way of compensation, it only uses half the quantity of steam per kWh compared with atmospheric exhaust plants. Technical advances have made it possible to generate electricity with fluid temperatures as low as 80–90°C.

The International Geothermal Association (IGA) estimates that worldwide electricity generating capacity from geothermal sources is over 8000 MWe producing 50 TWh per year. This is expected to rise to 11,400 MWe by 2005. In addition to this there is the direct heat energy production. The estimated ultimate potential for high temperature geothermal electricity is 36,600 TWh per year. For heat alone, the global estimate is 14 million TJ (IGA).

### Direct heat applications

As mentioned, medium- to low-temperature geothermal resources occur almost anywhere in the world and these have a use as sources of direct heat. Fifty-eight countries use geothermal energy in this way, amounting to an installed capacity of 15,145 MWt (thermal).

## Heat pumps

One of the most significant areas of application is in combination with heat pumps. There has been a rapid improvement in heat pump technology especially in the USA. At the time of writing it accounts for 12% of direct geothermal energy. Over the past few years the number of geothermal ground source heat pumps has grown by 59% with most of the expansion in the USA and Europe. Currently there are over half a million ground source heat pump installations in 26 countries.[1]

### Environmental impact

Despite claims to the contrary, it is virtually impossible to produce and transform energy without some carbon dioxide emissions. A survey of over 5000 MW installed capacity of geothermal emitted an average of 65 g carbon dioxide per kWh. This compares with 450 g/kWh for gas, 906 g/kWh for oil and 1042 g/kWh for coal, excluding the embodied energy in plant and equipment as well as carbon miles for the transportation of oil and coal. So, geothermal advocates are justified in their claim that it is one of the cleanest sources of energy.

At a guess, geothermal-boosted ground source heat pumps will lead the field in low-energy technology for buildings. It is relatively low cost, economical to run, insulated from the vagaries of weather and climate and changes in temperature and reliably produces heat in winter and cooling in summer. If PVs with battery backup provide the power for pumps and compressors then it really is a zero-energy system in operation.

Heat pumps are an offshoot of refrigeration technology. They exploit the principle that certain chemicals absorb heat when they are condensed into a liquid and release heat when they evaporate into a gas.

There are several different refrigerants that can be used for space heating and cooling with widely varying global warming potential (GWP). Refrigerants which have an ozone depleting potential are now banned. Currently refrigerants which have virtually zero GWP on release include ammonia which is one of the most prevalent.

The heating and cooling capacity of the refrigerant is enhanced by the extraction of warmth or 'coolth' from an external medium – earth, air or water.

The most efficient is the geothermal heat pump (GHP) which originated in the 1940s. This is another technology which goes back a long way but which is only now realizing its potential as a technology for the future. It exploits the relative warmth of the earth for both heating and cooling. The principle of the GHP is that it does not create heat; it transports it from one area to another. The main benefit of this technology is that it uses up to 50% less electricity than conventional electrical heating or cooling. A GHP uses one unit of electricity to move between three and four units of heat from the earth.

Most ground-coupled heat pumps adopt the closed-loop system whereby a high-density polyethylene pipe filled with a water and antifreeze mix that acts as a heat transporter is buried in the ground. It is laid in a U-configuration either vertically or horizontally. The vertical pipes descend to about a 100 m depth; the horizontal loop is laid at a minimum of 2 m depth.

The horizontal type is most common in residential situations where there is usually adequate open space and because it incurs a much lower excavation cost than the alternative. The only problem is that, even at a 2 m depth, the circuit can be affected by solar gain or rainfall evaporation. In each case the presence of moving ground water improves performance. Usually the lowest cost option is to use water in a pond, lake or river as the heat transfer medium. The supply pipe is run underground from the building and coiled into circles at least 1.75 m below the surface (see Fig. 4.2).

Dr Robin Curtis (GeoScience Ltd) considers heat pumps to be analogous to rechargeable batteries that are permanently connected to a trickle charger. The battery is the ground-loop array which has to be large enough, together with a matched compressor, to meet the heating/cooling load of a building. The energy trickle comes from the surrounding land which recharges the volume of ground immediately surrounding the loop. If the energy removed from the ground exceeds the ground's regeneration capacity, the system ceases to function, so it is essential that demand is matched to the ground capacity.

At present ground-coupled heat pumps have a coefficient of performance (COP) of between 3 and 4 which means that for every kilowatt of electricity they produce 3–4 kW of useful heat. The theoretical ultimate COP for heat pumps is 14. In the near future a COP of 8 is likely.

### Mode of operation of geothermal heat pumps

In the cooling mode a GHP is transformed into a refrigerator. Water circulating in the earth loop is warmer than the surrounding ground. It therefore releases heat to the ground, cooling in the process. The cooled water then passes through a heat exchanger in the heat pump. Within the heat exchanger refrigerant gas heated by a compressor releases its heat to the water which then begins its travel to release heat to the ground. The refrigerant having released its heat energy becomes a cold gas after passing through an expansion valve which is used to cool air or water. In a ducted air system the heat pump's fan circulates warm air from the building through the coils containing the cold refrigerant. The resultant cooled air is then blown through the ductwork of the building. The cold refrigerant

**Ground Coupled Heat Pumps (GCHP) a.k.a. closed loop heat pumps**

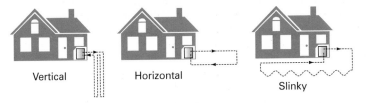

**Groundwater Heat Pumps (GWHP) a.k.a. open loop heat pumps**

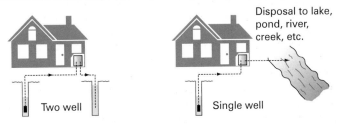

**Surface water Heat Pumps (SWHP) a.k.a. lake or pond loop heat pumps**

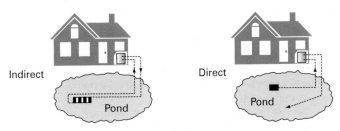

**Figure 4.2** Heat pump variations. (Source: Kensa Engineering.)

in the air coil picks up heat energy from the building and then travels to the compressor where it again becomes a hot gas and the cycle starts again.

A reversing valve linked to the compressor enables the heat pump to revert to a heating mode. In this case the water in the earth loop is colder than the surrounding ground and draws warmth from it. This heat is conveyed to the heat exchanger in the heat pump where the refrigerant absorbs heat from the water. The water leaves the heat exchanger to circulate through the earth and pick up more heat. The refrigerant, now converted to a gas having absorbed the heat from the earth loop, travels from the heat exchanger to the compressor. After compression the temperature of the refrigerant rises to about 65°C. It then passes to the building's heating distribution system which frequently comprises an underfloor hot water circuit.

**Figure 4.3** Ground source heat pumps in a commercial building context. (Source: *Geoscience.*)

After the refrigerant has released its heat it returns to the earth loop heat exchanger to start the cycle once more (see Fig. 4.3).

While heat pump technology has proved popular in the USA, it still has to establish itself in the UK. To help with this process a business park in Cornwall has just been completed that is exclusively heated by heat pumps supplied by Kensa Engineering of Falmouth. At present this seems to be the only company constructing heat pumps as opposed to importing them (see Fig. 4.4).

It is the Tolvaddon Energy Park which exploits geothermal energy with 19 heat pumps which pump water around boreholes to a depth of 70 m. The existence of this project is due to the support of the Regional Development Agency (RDA) for the South West and its insistence on the use of geothermal energy.

### Air-sourced air heat pumps

Instead of drawing warmth or coolth from a ground or water source, in warmer climes it is possible for the external source to be the air. In cooling mode the compressor pumps refrigerant to the outside coil where it condenses into a liquid. The air flowing across the coil removes heat from the refrigerant. It is then transported to the inside coil where it picks up heat from the interior of the building. Internal air is blown across the inside coil

**Figure 4.4**  Heat pump assembly at Kensa works.

where the liquid refrigerant evaporates giving up heat in the process. This cool air is blown into the building.

To provide heating the reversing valve in the pump directs refrigerant to the inside coil first. This makes the inside coil the condenser releasing heat to the interior duct system. The outside coil becomes the evaporator, collecting heat from the ambient air.

Air source heat pumps are becoming increasingly efficient. In fact, milder winters in the UK mean that inverter speed controlled compressors make air source heat pumps more efficient than ground source heat pumps. This version of the heat pump is mainly used to serve ducted air systems; there are very few available which operate wet underfloor heating systems. However, due to the absence of extensive external works, air source heat pumps are much cheaper than ground source systems.

### Variations

Rather than using electricity to power the compressor and fans, there is the prospect that natural gas or biofuel could be used to heat a Stirling engine to work the compressor and generate electricity for the fans. The excess heat could heat the building or provide domestic hot water.

There is also potential for heat from natural gas or biogas to supplement the output from the heat pump when the external temperature falls below

1.6°C. Such dual-fuel systems will be particularly attractive where gas prices are significantly lower than electricity costs.

## Sustainability

In certain locations the geothermal heat pump can reduce energy consumption and therefore carbon dioxide emissions by up to 72% compared with electric central heating and standard air-conditioning equipment.

Where ground coupled heat pumps are connected to the grid, given the present fuel mix across the European Union, this results in a 40% reduction in carbon dioxide emissions compared with modern fossil fuel alternatives. Add to this the fact that a ground loop lasts in excess of 50 years and the fact that heat pumps have high reliability and require no routine maintenance and the sustainability credentials of the technology are impressive.

## Economics

In terms of capital cost it is still the case that heat pumps are at a disadvantage as against fossil-fuel technologies. For example, the cost of a ground-source heat pump in the UK is at present two to three times that of a conventional fossil-fuel boiler. In the case of a resistive electric installation like electric underfloor heating the cost disparity is even greater. It is in running costs that the advantages are to be found. In more recently built, well-insulated homes with good thermal mass in the UK it is possible to achieve revenue savings as compared with mains gas, especially when maintenance costs are factored-in.

Things are better in the commercial sector. Where new low-energy buildings need both heating and cooling it is possible to demonstrate that ground-source heat pumps are competitive with conventional systems. This is because of cost savings in terms of reduced plantroom area, absence of fuel tanks, flues and gas connection. Capitalized running cost benefits also help to tip the balance in favour of heat pumps.

## Examples

Four elementary schools in Lincoln, Nebraska, USA installed geothermal heat pumps in 1996. In the first year of operation heating and cooling costs were $144,000 less than would have been incurred by conventional heating and cooling. In two other schools the total energy cost saving was 57%.

One of the most ambitious heat pump systems was installed in 1997 by Oslo International Airport. It uses a groundwater reservoir both for heat storage and a heat medium for the heat pumps and employs a circulating water rather than a closed-loop system. The installation has seven large piston compressors and uses ammonia as the cooling agent. In summer it provides a district cooling network which can reduce the temperature by

10°C compared with the external temperature. The total cooling capacity is 8.8 MW using 630 m$^3$ per hour of circulating water.

In heating mode 3 km of plastic pipe connect the energy centre with 18 wells, nine warm and nine cold. Water pumped from the warm to the cold wells works as a heat pump providing a temperature difference of 26°C equivalent to 8 MW of heat.

There are numerous advantages to heat pump technology that can be summarized as follows:

- Both heating and cooling are offered.
- It is environmentally friendly and could be zero carbon coupled to a renewable source of electricity such as PVs used to charge batteries to run the pumps. However, it would need a substantial PV array to produce at least 3 kW of electricity needed to power a heat pump.
- It is efficient (relatively high coefficient of performance) and uses less energy than conventional central heating and cooling systems to maintain indoor comfort conditions.
- Maintenance costs are virtually zero.
- It is versatile and can provide different zonal temperatures simultaneously and can, for example, move heat from computer rooms to perimeter rooms requiring extra heating.
- It is a highly durable technology because it has relatively few moving parts.
- It is quiet in operation.
- It can easily be retrofitted provided there already exists a low-temperature heating distribution system such as wet underfloor circuits. There is a problem for domestic retrofit in that homes in the UK normally have single-phase 230 V 50 Hz electricity supply. This limits the compressor size to 3 kW which in turn limits the heat pump capacity. Above this capacity heat pumps need a three-phase supply which, in the UK domestic market, would necessitate soft-start electric motors or an inverter.
- With underfloor wet systems the concrete floor slab insulated on the underside can act as a thermal store, enabling the heat pump to operate mainly on off-peak electricity.
- The heat output of a heat pump is purely conditioned by the size of the compressor.

With an accelerating demand for new housing in England, there is an ideal opportunity to exploit GHPs or water-sourced heat pumps on an ambitious scale. While the technology is generally more expensive to install than conventional heating systems, the payback time can be as little as 2 years with the bonus that maintenance costs are lower (US Department of Energy). They could be used to serve groups of houses or individually installed. A grouped scheme could have a single twin bore ground source serving heat pumps in each house.

Heat pumps are particularly appropriate for premises which need to dump heat, such as offices, hotels, restaurants, etc. In such circumstances payback time can be less than 5 years.

One difficulty with this technology is that it has an image problem. It is often perceived as a version of air-conditioning with all the environmental deficits which that implies.

Research is urgently needed into a standardized method of measuring the performance of heat pumps. Also there needs to be a cost-benefit analysis conducted across a wide range of samples across the European Union. We need to ask why heat pumps are much more in evidence in Sweden with its lower temperatures than in the UK.

## Note

1. Data from Lund JW and Freeston DH, World-wide direct use of geothermal energy 2000. *Geothermics* **30**, 29–68, 2001.

# 5 Wind power

The first known windmills were developed in Persia between 500 and 900 AD to pump water and grind grain. They consisted of vertical sails rotating round a central shaft. The first documented example of the technology in Europe dates from 1270. It shows a horizontal axis machine mounted on a central post with four sails, known predictably as a 'post-mill' machine. It took until the nineteenth century for the windmill sails to achieve peak efficiency. These sails had some of the crucial features which helped in the design of present-day turbine blades.

Between 1983 and 2000 the growth of installed wind-generating capacity almost followed an exponential curve. In the year 2000 there was 14.6% more installed capacity than in the previous year bringing the world total for the year to 4495 MW. Of that total 86% was in Europe. BTM Consult state the world total capacity by the end of 2000 was 18,449 MW generated by 49,238 wind turbines.[1] The BTM report also predicts that European wind energy will reach 40–60 GW by 2010.

Compared with other renewable energy technologies, wind energy is the closest to being competitive with fossil-based systems. The technology is mature and robust, with offshore installations set to take off in Europe. These facts should dispel any uncertainty about the future role of wind in the energy scenarios of the twenty-first century.

This chapter is mainly concerned with small-scale wind generation that can operate as embedded generation in buildings and this is where some of the most interesting developments have taken place. In this context 'small' means wind machines that are scaled from a few watts to 20 kW. Machines between 1 and 5 kW may be used to provide either direct current (DC) or alternating current (AC). They are mainly confined to the domestic level and are often used to charge batteries. The larger machines are suitable for commercial/industrial buildings and groups of houses.

Small-scale electricity production on site has economic disadvantages in the UK given the present New Electricity Trading Arrangement (NETA). Presently, government is considering how to redress this inequity and thereby give a substantial boost to the market for small-scale renewables. Wind generation will do well if this happens since it is much less expensive in terms of installed cost per kilowatt than PV which makes it an attractive proposition as a building integrated power source.

Wind patterns in the built environment are complex as the air passes over, around and between buildings. Accordingly a wind generator introduced into this environment must be able to cope with high turbulence caused by buildings. Such conditions tend to favour vertical axis machines as opposed to the horizontal versions which have proliferated in wind farms. This is because the vertical versions may be able to operate at lower wind speeds and they are less stressed mechanically by turbulence. In addition, horizontal axis machines mounted on roofs tend to transmit vibrations through the structure of the buildings. Because of the bending moment produced by the tower under wind load, measures must be taken to provide adequate strength in the building structure. This is not easily achieved in retrofit situations.

By their very nature the vertical axis machines are not affected by changes in wind direction or turbulence. They can be sited on roofs or walls. They have been particularly successful mounted on the sides of oil platforms in the North Sea (see Fig. 5.1).

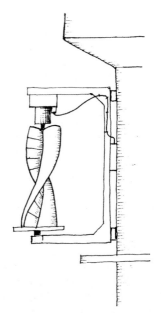

**Figure 5.1** Helical side mounted turbine on oil platform.

The machines are well balanced, transmitting minimum vibration and bending stress to walls or roofs. They also have a high output power-to-weight ratio. A further advantage is that the electricity generator is located beneath the rotors and therefore can be located within the envelope of the building.

Wind generation can be complemented by PVs by the system patented by Altechnica. The wind generators continue operating at night when PVs are in retirement (see Fig. 5.7).

A projection by *WIND Directions* (March 2001) estimates that the global market for small turbines by 2005 will be around €173 million and several hundreds of million by 2010. For example, in the Netherlands alone there is the potential for 20,000 urban turbines to be installed on industrial and commercial buildings by 2011.

The increasing deregulation of the energy market creates an increasingly attractive proposition for independent off-grid small-scale generation insulating the operator from price fluctuations and reliability uncertainties, with the proviso that there is a level playing field in the market.

Presently, there are several versions of vertical axis machines available. However, they are still undergoing development. When it is fully appreciated that these machines are reliable, silent, low maintenance, easy to install and competitive on price, it is likely the market will expand rapidly. At present the regulatory regime for small turbines is much less onerous than for >20 kW machines. It is to be hoped that the bureaucrats fail to spot this red tape opportunity.

Research conducted by Delft University of Technology and Ecofys identified five building conditions to determine their effectiveness for wind turbines. Four are described as 'wind catchers', 'wind collectors', 'wind sharers' and 'wind gatherers', terms which define their effect on wind speed. The wind catcher is well suited to small turbines being usually high and benefiting from a relatively free wind flow. Small horizontal axis machines could be satisfactory in this situation.

The wind collector type of building has a lower profile and can be subject to turbulence. This is where the vertical axis machine comes into its own. The third type, wind sharers, are found in industrial areas and business parks. Their relatively even roof height and spaced out siting makes such buildings subject to high winds and turbulence. Ecofys has produced a diagram which depicts how four urban situations cope with varying wind conditions. There is a fifth category, the 'Winddreamer' which relates to low rise developments (see Fig. 5.2).

Development work is continuing on designs for turbines which are suitable for the difficult wind conditions found in urban situations. This is appropriate since climate change predictions indicate that wind speeds will increase as the atmosphere heats up and so becomes more dynamic. There is growing confidence that there will be a large market for mini-turbines in various configurations on offices, housing blocks and individual dwelling.

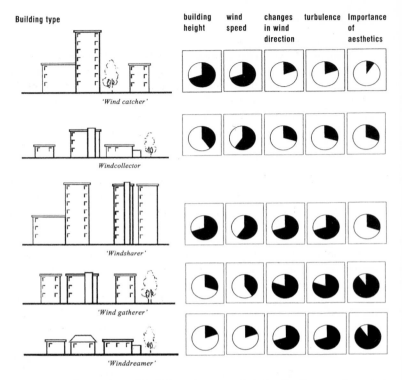

**Figure 5.2** Categories of building cluster and their effectiveness for wind generation. (Courtesy of Ecofys and *Renewable Energy World*.)

## Types of small-scale wind turbine

Most small systems have a direct drive permanent magnet generator that limits mechanical transmission losses. Systems under 2 kW usually have a 24–48 V capacity aimed at battery charging or a DC circuit rather than having grid compatibility.

Up to the now, horizontal axis machines are much more in evidence than the vertical axis type even at this scale. These machines have efficient braking systems for when wind speed is excessive. Some even tip backwards in high winds adopting the so-called 'helicopter position'. There are advantages to horizontal axis machines such as:

- the cost benefit due to economy of scale of production
- it is a robust and tested technology
- automatic start-up
- high output.

The disadvantages are:

- the necessity of a high mast
- when mounted on buildings they require substantial foundation support
- in urban situations where there can be large variations in wind direction and speed, this necessitates frequent changes of orientation and blade speed; this not only undermines power output it also increases the dynamic loading on the machine with consequent wear and tear
- there are noise problems with this kind of machine especially associated with braking in high winds
- they can be visually intrusive.

As stated earlier, vertical axis turbines are particularly suited to urban situations and to being integrated into buildings. They are discrete and virtually silent and much less likely to trigger the wrath of planning officials. This type has even been the basis for an art work as in a sports stadium at Yurigoaka, Japan.

A problem with some very small vertical axis machines is that they need mechanical start-up which can be achieved either by an electric motor or a link to a Savonius-type rotor. The most common vertical axis machine is the helical turbine as seen at the Earth Centre, Doncaster (see Fig. 5.3). In that instance it is mounted on a tower but it can also be side-hung on a building. Another variety is the S-Rotor which has an S-shaped blade.

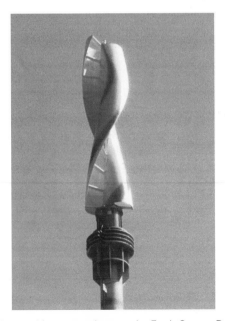

**Figure 5.3**   Helican turbine on a column at the Earth Centre, Doncaster.

The Darrieus-Rotor employs three slender elliptical blades which can be assisted by a wind deflector. This is an elegant machine that nevertheless needs start-up assistance. A variation of the genre is the H-Darrieus-Rotor with triple vertical blades extending from the central axis. Yet another configuration is the Lange turbine which has three sail-like wind scoops (see Fig. 5.4). Last in this group is the 'Spiral flugel' turbine in which twin blades create, as the name indicates, a spiral partnership (see Fig. 5.5).

Returning to the horizontal axis machines, a development from the 1970s has placed the turbine blades inside an aerofoil cowling. A prototype developed at the University of Rijeka, Croatia, claims that this combination can produce electricity 60% more of the time compared with conventional machines. This is because the aerofoil concentrator enables the machines to produce electricity at slower wind speeds than is possible with conventional turbines.

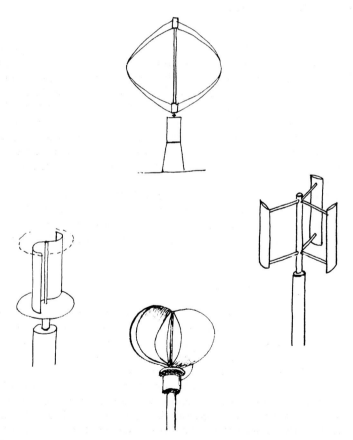

**Figure 5.4**  *Left*: S-Rotor; *top centre*: Darrieus-Rotor; *bottom centre*: Lange turbine; *right*: H-Darrieus-Rotor.

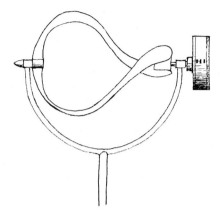

**Figure 5.5** Spiral Flugel rotor.

The cross-section of the cowling has a profile similar to the wing of an aircraft which creates an area of low pressure inside the cowling. This has the effect of accelerating the air over the turbine blades. As a result, more electricity is produced for a given wind speed as well as generating at low air speeds. This amplification of wind speed has its hazards in that blades can be damaged. The answer has been to introduce hydraulically driven air release vents into the cowling which are activated when the pressure within the cowling is too great. They also serve to stabilize electricity output in turbulent wind conditions, which makes them appropriate for urban sites.

This technology can generate power from 1 kW to megawatt capacity. It is being considered for offshore application. The device is about 75% more expensive than conventional rotors but the efficiency of performance is improved by a factor of five as against a conventional horizontal axis turbine (see Fig. 5.6).

## Building integrated systems

There is increasing interest in the way that the design of buildings can incorporate renewable technologies including wind turbines. Up to now such machines have been regarded as adjunct to buildings but a concept patented by Altechnica of Milton Keynes demonstrates how multiple turbines can become a feature of the design.

The system is designed to be mounted on the ridge of a roof or at the apex of a curved roof section. Rotors are incorporated in a cage-like structure which is capped with an aerofoil wind concentrator called in this case a 'solairfoil'. The flat top of the solairfoil can accommodate PVs. Where the rotors are mounted at the apex of a curved roof the affect is to concentrate the wind in a manner similar to the Croatian cowling (see Fig. 5.7).

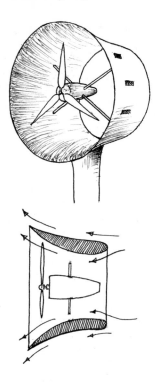

**Figure 5.6**   Wind turbine with cowling wind concentrator.

The advantage of this system is that it does not become an over-assertive visual feature and is perceived as an integral design element. It is also a system that can easily be fitted to existing buildings where the wind regime is appropriate. Furthermore it indicates a building which is discretely capturing the elements and working for a living. Altechnica has also illustrated how small-scale rotors can be incorporated into the design of a

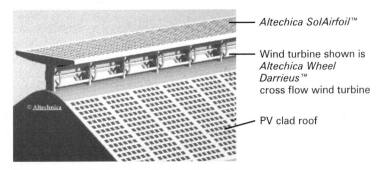

Altechica SolAirfoil™

Wind turbine shown is
*Altechica Wheel
Darrieus™*
cross flow wind turbine

PV clad roof

**Figure 5.7**   'Aeolian' roof devised by Altechnica.

high building. This approach has been demonstrated by Bill Dunster Architects in their SkyZed concept.

This is a multi-storey residential block consisting of four lobes which, on plan, resemble the petals of a flower, hence its colloquial name the 'flower-tower'. The curved floor plates serve to accelerate the wind by up to a factor of four at the core of the building. Here vertical axis generators are positioned at every fourth floor. This is the only type of turbine appropriate for this situation being virtually silent in operation. Also at every fourth floor there are access platforms linking the accommodation lobes and serving as platforms to view the rotors. This building will be considered in more detail as a case study (see Fig 15.17 and 15.18, and www.zedfactory.com).

Finally, the subject of wind power cannot be left without reference to changes in distribution technology which are likely to come increasingly in evidence as offshore wind farms are developed at ever greater distances from land. It concerns transporting electricity as medium to high voltage DC current instead of the conventional AC. As distances from the shore increase from the present 5–15 to 50–200 km, AC cables become increasingly inefficient. At a distance of 100 km AC cables use so much electricity generating heat that at the destination there is virtually no usable power. The principle is that the AC current generated by the turbines is converted to high-voltage DC for transportation and then back to AC in a conversion terminal onshore. By changing to DC transportation the theoretical transport capacity of existing lines could be increased by a factor of two. This switch has been made economic by the introduction of DC transformers, powerful switches and custom-developed safety and protection devices.

This DC conversion technology offers great advantages in urban situations whenever it becomes necessary to enlarge the capacity of the existing grid. Medium-voltage DC (MVDC) technology involves raising the cable voltage and this can be done with existing AC cables without having to expose the cables. Thus the curse of all urban dwellers, the digging up of roads, could be considerably curtailed.

The European Commission White Paper on Renewable Sources of Energy set a goal of 12% penetration of renewables across the Union by 2010. Within this target the goal for wind energy is 40 GW of installed power producing 8 TWh of electricity. This would save 72 million tonnes of carbon dioxide per year. The European Wind Energy Association considers this to be conservative since current growth rates suggest that a target of 60 GW is feasible. That would mean that by 2020 wind would account for almost 10% of all European Union electricity production.

Another important statistic is that the latest version of a 600 kW turbine will save between 20,000 and 36,000 tonnes of carbon dioxide over its 20-year life. The difference is due to varying site and wind conditions. As yet the cost benefit of such a technology in terms of avoided damage to the biosphere, human health, plant damage, etc. is not acknowledged in the price regime. However, the European Union Extern-E study has sought to put a price on the damage inflicted by fossil fuels compared with wind energy. The research has concluded that, for 40 GW of wind power installed by 2010, and with a total investment of €24.8 billion up to 2010, carbon dioxide emissions could be reduced by 54 million tonnes per year in the final year. The cumulative saving would amount to 320 million tonnes of carbon dioxide giving avoided external costs of up to €15 billion.

This is the first sign of a revolution in the way of accounting for energy. When the avoided costs of external damage are realistically factored-in to the cost of fossil fuels, the market should have no difficulty in switching to renewable energy *en masse*.

## Note

1.  Data from the 'World Market Update 2000 Report' from BTM Consult which produces statistics on an annual basis.

# 6 Photovoltaic cells

Electricity is produced from solar energy when photons or particles of light are absorbed by semi-conductors. This is the basis of the photovoltaic (PV) cell.

Most solar cells in present use are built from solid-state semiconducting material. Semiconductors are at the centre of the electronic revolution of the last century and it is worth a moment to consider how they function.

Silicon is a typical semiconductor material in that its electrical properties can be influenced in a number of ways. The electronic structure of a solid, that is, the disposition of its electrons, falls into bands separated by 'band gaps'. A flow of electrons represents an electric current. The ability of electrons to move is determined by the extent to which a particular band is filled. Electrons in filled bands are relatively static. So solids with fully filled bands cannot conduct electricity; there is no space to allow electrons to move. Such materials are insulators. Materials with partially filled bands like most metals are conductors.

In all solids the saturated electronic band that has the highest energy density is called the 'valence band'. The next band above the valence band is the 'conduction band'. In insulators this band is empty; in metals, partially filled. The electronic band structure of silicon is similar to that of insulators. The valence band is completely filled and conduction band empty. What distinguished a semiconductor from a pure insulator is the size of the band gap. In silicon it is small enough for a few electrons in the valence band to pick up enough thermal energy to hop into the conduction band where they have the space to move. This leaves a vacancy or hole in the valence band which has a real existence with an electrical charge opposite to that of an electron. It is, in effect, a virtual particle. So, in silicon, an electrical current is carried by a few energetic particles in the conduction band moving in one direction and by positively charged 'holes' in the valence bands moving in the opposite direction. This movement of particles is activated by the application of heat. The charged particles are thermally excited.

The conductivity of semiconductors can be improved by the addition of certain foreign atoms that provide additional charge carriers. These atoms are called 'dopants'. In the case of silicon, an atom of arsenic replacing an atom of silicon results in the material acquiring an extra electron. The valence band being full means that this extra electron sits within the band gap which in turn means that it takes less energy to enable it to gravitate to the conduction band. In other words it more readily becomes a thermally excited charge carrier. This kind of doping introduces negative charge carriers hence its description 'n-type' doping.

Conversely using a dopant that has one fewer valence electrons than silicon creates a hole in the valence band. This hole behaves as a positive charge carrier. This is described as p-type doping. This manipulation of the electronic properties of silicon by doping has provided the basis of silicon microelectronics. At the heart of this technology is the so-called p-n junction or interface.

In the case of photovoltaic cells a layer of semiconductor material lies back to back with another semiconductor. One is p-doped and the other n-doped. This sets up an electrical field at the interface. When light falls on the cell, the energy from the photons frees some electrons in the semiconductors which are propelled to the extremities of the two-layer structure. This creates a difference in potential which generates an electrical current. Metal electrodes are attached to the two faces of the cell to complete an electrical circuit (see Fig. 6.1).

At present in most cells the p- and n-doped cells are formed within a monolithic piece of crystalline silicon. To reduce efficiency loss through reflection, most crystalline cells are chemically etched to roughen the surface. The absorption bandwidth of these cells is from 350 nm, the ultra-

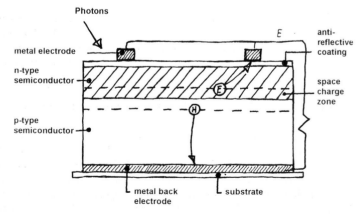

**Figure 6.1**  Crystalline silicon photovoltaic cell.

violet part of the spectrum, to the near infrared 1.1 $\mu$m. The fundamental conversion efficiency limit of crystalline silicon is said to be 29%.

A characteristic of such cells is that heat is generated when electrons are propelled to the boundary of the n-doped semi-conductor, heat which needs to be dissipated, otherwise the efficiency of the cell is reduced.

## Crysalline and amorphous silicon cells

Less efficient, but cheaper to produce are silicon-based cells which do not have a crystalline atomic structure. Hydrogenated amorphous silicon (a-Si:H) comprising a thin film 0.5 $\mu$m thick forms the basis of highly light absorbant cells hence the description 'thin film solar cell'. They are produced by atomic deposition over a large area and consequently much more economical to produce than crystalline silicon cells which involve slicing up slabs of crystalline silicon grown by a slow crystallization process.

The efficiency of this technology has been improved by stacking cells which capture light at different wavelengths. Different alloys of silicon capture the blue, green and red/infrared parts of the spectrum. A triple junction terrestrial concentrator solar cell has been produced by Spectrolab Inc of the USA which has achieved an efficiency in the laboratory of 34%. The variations in the silicon are:

- top: amorphous silicon alloy (a-Si alloy) – blue
- middle: a-Si + 10% germanium – green
- bottom: a-Si + 40–50% germanium – red/infrared.

Light passes through all three layers and is reflected back by a silver/zinc oxide reflector. The cells are able to withstand highly concentrated sunlight and using a concentrator reduces the number of cells needed to produce a given amount of electricity.

## Dye-based cells

The dominance of silicon is being challenged by a new generation of solar cells that mimic the process of photosynthesis. Developed by Michael Gratzel and Brian O'Regan of the University of Lausanne, this cell uses a dye containing ruthenium ions that absorb visible light analogous to chlorophyll in nature. The dye is applied to nanocrystals of the semi-conductor titanium dioxide or 'titania'. The titania has the electronic property of being able to draw electrons from the ruthenium and propel them off into an electrical circuit.

The construction of the cell involves sandwiching a 10-$\mu$m thick film of dye-coated titania between two transparent electrodes. The tightly packed nanocrystals form a porous film that maximizes the light absorbing capacity of the cell. The space between the electrodes is filled with a liquid electrolyte containing iodine ions. These ions replace those knocked out of the dye by the action of the photons. The two electrodes are connected to form a circuit that carries the electrical discharge (see Fig. 6.2).

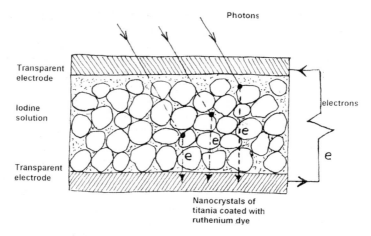

**Figure 6.2**   Titanium-ruthenium dye-coated PV cell.

The conversion efficiency is around 10% in direct sunlight but up to 15% in the diffuse light of cloudy days which makes these cells especially suitable for northern climes. The cost is claimed to be only 20% of the price of crystalline silicon, and may be even less since huge deposits of titanium have been discovered in Australia.

Solar cells which are transparent is the solution to the wider application of façade PVs. This means creating cells which can produce a significant amount of electricity by absorbing light only in the infrared end of the spectrum. These would be coated with a dye that is transparent yet absorbs light in this invisible part of the spectrum. Michael Gratzel of the University of Lausanne considers that such cells could achieve a conversion rate of 10%.[1]

## Monolithic tandem concentrator cells

The Fraunhofer Institute for Solar Energy in Freiburg has developed a PV based on a thin-film structure of two semiconductors: gallium indium arsenide and gallium indium phosphide. Solar concentrators are incorporated in the cell which increases the solar intensity by factors ranging from 100 to 1000. Because the optical concentrators focus solar energy onto a small area, this reduces the area of cells required for a given output. In the laboratory the cells achieve an efficiency of 29%, but values up to 35% are expected to result from further developments. The disadvantage of this technology is that the concentrators are really only efficient in sunlight.

## Flexible solar panels

Shell Renewables and Akzo Nobel in the Netherlands are jointly developing a low-cost process for mass producing flexible solar cell panels. A special semiconductor coating is applied to rolls of flexible foil substrate on an almost continuous basis. The process is being developed in parallel by the Technical Universities of Delft and Eindhoven, Utrecht University, the Energy Research Centre of the Netherlands, NOVEM the Dutch agency for energy and the environment and the European Union. This technology promises to be ideal for roof and wall panel application.

Other PV technologies include cadmium telluride (CdTe) cells being developed in the US (BP Solar) and Germany (Siemens) (see p. 151). This promises to be in production in Germany by 2003. First Solar in the US has developed a 100 MW CdTe coating facility and a 25 MW module fabrication plant. The process deposits CdTe on glass with a transparent conducting oxide. Modules of 0.75 $m^2$ will be produced by a plant in 2002. The efficiency is modest at 8% but, in compensation, the cost is low combined with the fact that it can be employed as roof and wall covering. The main disadvantage is that cadmium is a highly toxic metal.

The Boeing Corporation has developed a gallium arsenide thin film cell which can achieve high absorption rates. A single junction cell has realized 28.7% efficiency, while a tandem two-junction cell has reached 33%.

Siemens has focused on a copper indium diselenide (CIS) cell with an efficiency of 9–11%.

An innovative technology has been developed by Daystar Inc of Denver, Colorado, USA. It employs 1-mm diameter filaments of polycrystalline copper indium gallium diselenide (CIGs) as a semi-conductor deposited on stainless steel wires. Light is focused onto the wires by built-in elliptical lenses. The cost of materials is claimed to be one-fifth that of silicon cells and peak efficiency is said to be 18% (www.daystartech.com/products.htm).

Finally, scientists at Cambridge University are developing an organic cell which uses two different types of carbon molecule, which, when mixed together, separate into layers and start converting light to electricity. So far the device has achieved 34% efficiency but only in the blue–green part of the spectrum. The objective is to encompass the whole spectrum. This would seem to be a technology to watch.

## Photovoltaics: cost projections

Some governments have intervened to enable PVs to achieve economies of scale, notably Germany, the USA and Japan. A combination of subsidies, market growth and technical gains promises to deliver sharp reductions in cost. A tripling of annual production would bring PV prices down to the level of conventional power. It is likely that the domestic market will provide the impetus for this expansion. The key to success will be the production of roof and wall systems that compete with conventional materials.

### Projections of PV market penetration

A joint research project by the European Photovoltaic Industry Association (EPIA) and Greenpeace has produced an estimate of the development of

PVs to 2020 and 2040 (*Solar Generation*). The EPIA represents 52 of Europe's leading PV companies.

The report estimates that the output of PV will rise from the 280 MWp in 2000 to over 40,000 MWp in 2020 producing about 274 TWh world-wide. This would account for 30% of Africa's needs. This assumes that:

- the market development over recent years is maintained
- there are national and regional support programmes
- there are national targets for PV installations and manufacturing capacity
- suitable sites are available including roofs
- there is a growth in demand from areas not grid connected.

The International Energy Agency predicts that world electricity demand by 2020 will be 26,000 TWh with an installed capacity of 195 GWp. About half the world would be grid connected, mostly in the industrialized countries. Assuming 80% of demand will be from homes with an average demand of 3 kW serving three people, by 2020 the total generating their own electricity would be 82 million, with 35 million in Europe being grid connected.

In developing countries the capacity by 2020 is expected to be 30 GWp, of which 10 GW will be used for homes with an average demand of 50 Wp. This would amount to one million using PV.

The overall effect would be to reduce carbon dioxide emissions by 164 million tonnes at the same time creating an employment potential of two million jobs.

By 2040, assuming:

- a 15% p.a. growth in PV
- the lifetime of PVs of 20 years
- power consumption increasing from 26,000 TWh in 2020 to 35,000 TWh

then solar PV will account for 7368 TWh or 23% of world electricity output.

## Photovoltaics and urban design

Towns and cities present an ideal opportunity for the exploitation of PVs. They have a high concentration of potential PV sites with a heavy energy demand. At the same time the physical infrastructure can support localized electricity generation. It is estimated that installing PV on suitable walls and roofs could generate up to 25% of total demand.

It is worth noting that solar irradiation in Malmo, Sweden is higher than in southern England and only 20% less than Florence despite the difference in latitude. The biggest potential for PV is as systems embedded in buildings. It is expected that building integrated PV (BIPV) will account for 50% of the world PV installations by 2010, with the percentage being significantly higher in Europe.

The widescale adoption of PV in the urban environment will depend on the acceptance of the visual change it will bring about, especially in historic situations. There is still a barrier to be overcome and planning policy guidance may have to be amended to create a presumption in favour of retrofitting PV to buildings.

The efficiency of PV in a given location will depend on several factors such as:

* compact developments with fairly consistent roof heights are ideal for roof-mounted PVs
* orientation is an important factor
* a more open urban grain may exploit the potential of façade PV: in this case overshading must be considered especially in the context of seasonal changes in the sun's angle.

Nieuwland, near Amersfoort in the Netherlands, is a new town in which building integrated PVs is a feature of many homes producing a peak total of 1.3 MW (see Fig. 6.3).

A way of measuring the effectiveness of the urban massing to accommodate PVs is the 'sky view factor' (SVF) devised by Koen Steemers and colleagues at the Martin Centre in the University of Cambridge. This gives an indication of the spacing between buildings and indicates the amount of the sky which is visible from any particular position in a city whether at street or roof level. A totally unobstructed situation has a value of 1. Steemers gives two examples: a medieval part of Athens and Grugliasco in Italy. The average SVF from the streets for Athens is 0.68 and for Grugliasco 0.82 (see Fig. 6.4).

**Figure 6.3**  The new town of Nieuwland near Amersfoort. (Courtesy of Ecofys and *Renewable Energy World*.)

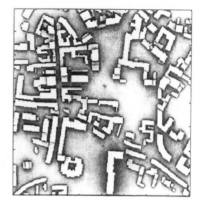

**Figure 6.4** Sky view factor for two towns: medieval Athens (*left*) and Grugliasco, Italy (*right*). (Source: The Martin Centre, Cambridge.)

The intensity of the grey indicates the degree of visible sky with white being the SVF of 1. In Athens the buildings are tightly packed at high density and so the streets offer few opportunities for façade BIPVs. On the other hand, there is a relatively even overall building height that creates a good situation for roof PVs. In contrast, the Italian example has a smaller overall area of roof but light shading at street level and therefore opportunities for façade BIPV.

### Surface-to-volume ratio

The surface area available for either façade or roof PV installation is largely determined by the surface-to-volume ratio. A high ratio of surface to volume suggests opportunities for façade integrated PVs. However, in high density situations overshading will limit facade opportunities. On the other hand, lower values indicate opportunities for roof PVs. In the examples from Steemers the lighter the shading the more the PV opportunities. The lower the value the greater the potential for roof-mounted PVs (see Fig. 6.5).

As stated, the spacing between buildings is an important factor in determining façade PV opportunities Figure 6.6 shows three plan orientations coupled with three height-to-width ratios. The street with west-to-east façades offers the least overall efficiency for solar access, whereas the diagonal street offers the best overall solar opportunity. However, to sum up, wide spacing between buildings with a southerly aspect will be particularly suited to façade BIPV. Wide streets and city square provide excellent opportunities for this PV mode. A tighter urban grain points to roof-mounted PVs.

The relationship between urban form and PV potential has been demonstrated by comparing four urban configurations all with a plot ratio of 1.7. Figure 6.7 shows how the percentage of façade area with annual irradiation of >800 kWh/m$^2$ varies with building type and location. The tower

**Figure 6.5** Comparative surface-to-volume ratios for European cities. (a) West Cambridge, UK (SSC: 20%, S/V: 0.27). (b) Fribourg/Freiburg, Switzerland (SSC: 21%, S/V: 0.24). (c) Trondheim (present), Norway (SSC: 29%, S/V: 0.23). (d) Trondheim (proposed), Norway (SSC: 36%, S/V: 0.14). (e) Athens (old part), Greece (SSC: 49%, S/V: 0.31). (f) Athens (modern), Greece (SSC: 51%, S/V: 0.25). (g) Grugliasco (old part), Italy (SSC: 30%, S/V: 0.35). (h) Grugliasco (modern), Italy (SSC: 19%, S/V: 0.28). (SSC = sites surface coverage, S/V = surface/volume) (Source: The Martin Centre, Cambridge.)

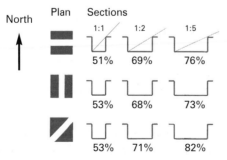

**Figure 6.6** Solar access and space between buildings. (Source: The Martin Centre, Cambridge.)

| Urban area (plot ratio = 1.7) | | Climate | Percentage of façade and annual irradiation c. 800 kVV |
|---|---|---|---|
| Pavilion-Court |  | Athens | **30%** |
| | | Torino | 17% |
| | | Fribourg | 6% |
| | | Cambridge | 2% |
| | | Tronheim | 24% |
| Pavilion |  | Athens | **13%** |
| | | Torino | 4% |
| | | Fribourg | 1% |
| | | Cambridge | 6% |
| | | Tronheim | 39% |
| Slab |  | Athens | **39%** |
| | | Torino | 23% |
| | | Fribourg | 7% |
| | | Cambridge | 2% |
| | | Tronheim | 39% |
| Terrace |  | Athens | **50%** |
| | | Torino | 38% |
| | | Fribourg | 11% |
| | | Cambridge | 2% |
| | | Tronheim | 14% |

**Figure 6.7**   Percentage of façade receiving solar radiation in four configurations. (Source: The Martin Centre, Cambridge.)

layout (pavilions) is the least efficient whereas the terraces offer the best exposure.

In conclusion, the suitability of BIPV is dependent on a variety of factors. For example, flat roofs are the most appropriate sites in city centres, combining flexibility with unobtrusiveness.

In considering pitched roofs, the orientation, angle of tilt and aesthetic impact all have to be taken into account.

Reflected light is a useful supplemental form of energy for PVs. Many façades in city centres have high reflectance values offering significant levels of diffuse light for façade PV on opposite elevations, thus making orientation less important.

In glazed curtain wall buildings solar shading is now *de rigueur.* Here is a further opportunity to incorporate PV into shading devices. When office blocks are refurbished the incorporation of PV into a façade becomes highly cost effective.

In conservation areas there are particular sensitivities. The next generation of thin-film PVs look like offering opportunities to integrate PVs into buildings without compromising their historic integrity.

## Note

1.  *New Scientist*, 23 January 1999, p. 40.

# 7 Fuel cells

It has taken since 1839, when Sir William Grove invented the technology, for the fuel cell to be recognized as the likely principal power source of the future. It is the fuel cell that will be the bridge between the hydrocarbon economy and hydrogen-based society. David Hart who is head of fuel cells and hydrogen research at Imperial College has no doubt about the possibilities for fuel cells:

> *If fuel cells fulfil their potential, there's no reason why they shouldn't replace almost every battery and combustion engine in the world.*[1]

There is still considerable potential for improvements in the efficiency of fuel cells since they are not dependent on heat *per se* but on electrochemical conversion which means they are not limited by the second law of thermodynamics.

Until recently one reason for scepticism about the technology was the cost. However, since 1989 there has been a dramatic fall in cost per kilowatt of output (see Fig. 7.1).

System developers are confident that cost will fall to $300–500 per kW installed capacity for stationary application, mostly due to economies of scale.

In the USA there is considerable activity in fuel cell development, not least because of the Department of Energy's (DoE) upbeat stance over the technology:

> *The vision is staggering: a society powered almost entirely by hydrogen, the most abundant element in the universe … The overall goal of the DoE is to replace two to four quads of conventional energy with hydrogen by the year 2010, and replace 10 quads per year by 2030. A quad is the amount of energy consumed by one million households.*

So, what is it about the fuel cell that gets people so excited?

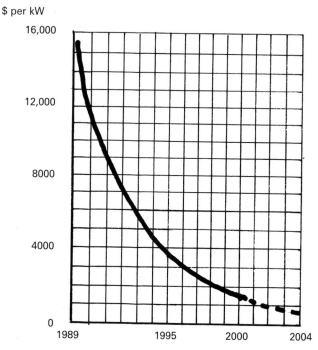

**Figure 7.1** Improving economics of fuel cells. (Based on data from *New Scientist*, 25 November 2000.)

Fuel cells are electrochemical devices that generate direct current (DC) electricity similar to batteries. Unlike batteries they require a continual input of a hydrogen-rich fuel. They have been described as electrochemical internal combustion engines. In essence the fuel cell is a reactor which combines hydrogen and oxygen to produce electricity, heat and water. It is a robust technology with few moving parts. It is clean, quiet and emits no pollution when fed directly with hydrogen.

At the outset it should be useful to provide a glossary of terms associated with this technology.

- *Anode*. Electrode at which an oxidation reaction takes place
- *Bipolar plates*. Plates used to connect fuel cells in series to form a stack and build up voltage. They can be made of steel, graphite or conducting polymer. The plates are designed to facilitate gas distribution to each cell of the stack; to assist cooling, fluids separation and distribution; electrical conduction and physical support. Flow channels are carved into the plates to allow an even distribution of hydrogen and oxygen to the cells.
- *Catalyst*. Molecule, metal or other chemical substance used to increase the rate of a reaction. The catalyst takes part in the reaction mechanism without being consumed by the reactants.

- *Cathode*. Electrode at which a reduction reaction takes place.
- *Cogeneration*. The utilization of both electrical and thermal energy from a power plant.
- *Electrode*. Electric conductor through which a flow of electrons is created (an electrical current). An electrochemical system has a minimum of two: an anode and a cathode that are in direct contact with the electrolyte.
- *Electrolyte*. A substance, solid or liquid, that conducts ions between electrodes in an electrochemical cell. The electrolyte is in direct contact with the electrodes.
- *Energy density*. The amount of available energy per unit weight or volume of the power plant.
- *Exothermic reaction*. A chemical reaction that releases heat.
- *Ion-exchange membrane*. A thin film that allows ion conduction and separation of fuel (e.g. hydrogen) at the anode and oxidant (air) at the cathode. Another term for electrolyte.
- *Matrix*. The electrolyte-containing layer between the anode and cathode of the fuel cell. Generally fuel cells are classified by their electrolyte. One of the most common types of cell is the polymer electrolyte membrane fuel cell, which is considered in the next section.

## Polymer electrolyte membrane fuel cell (PEMFC)

Sometimes called the proton exchange membrane fuel cell (PEMFC in either case) it is also referred to as the solid polymer fuel cell. This is one of the most common types of cell being appropriate for both vehicle and static application. Of all the cells in production it has the lowest operating temperature of 80°C. The cell consists of an anode and a cathode separated by an electrolyte, in this case usually Teflon. Both the anode and cathode are coated with platinum which acts as a catalyst. Hydrogen is fed to the anode and an oxidant (oxygen from the air) to the cathode. The catalyst on the anode causes the hydrogen to split into its constituent protons and electrons. The electrolyte membrane allows only protons to pass through to the cathode setting up a charge separation in the process. The electrons pass through an external circuit creating useful energy at around 0.7 volts then recombining with protons at the cathode to produce water (see Fig. 7.2).

To build up a useful voltage cells are stacked between conductive bipolar plates, usually graphite which have integral channels to allow the free flow of hydrogen and oxygen (see Fig. 7.3)

The electrical efficiency of the PEMFC is 35% with a target of 45%. Its energy density is 0.3 kW/kg compared with 1.0 kW/kg for internal combustion engines.

One problem with the PEMFC is that it requires hydrogen of a high degree of purity. Research activity is focusing on finding cheaper and more robust catalysts as well as more efficient ion exchange polymer electrolytes.

Originally the PEMFCs were conceived for vehicle application. Now they are being developed to supply single homes or housing estates with

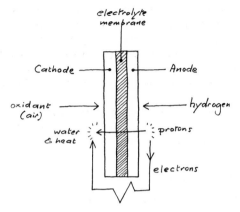

**Figure 7.2**   Polymer Electrolyte or Proton Exchange Membrane fuel cell.

electricity and heat. Approximately the same amount of heat and electricity are generated. Initially the hydrogen fuel will be obtained from reformed natural gas supplied through existing networks. Rather optimistically an editorial in the *New Scientist* November 2000 predicted that 'Within a couple of years, fuel cells will provide heat and power for homes and offices'. It goes on to suggest that cheap gas will enable fuel cells 'to undercut today's combination of heating boiler and mains electricity'. It is more likely that 2005 will be the date by which fuel cell combined heat and power will start to penetrate the domestic market.

However, it has already penetrated the sphere of transport. Buses in the city of Vancouver have been operating Ballard PEMFCs since 1993. The cells deliver 125 hp and the buses have a range of 100 miles. The Chicago Transit Authority hopes to substitute this technology for all its 2000 buses.

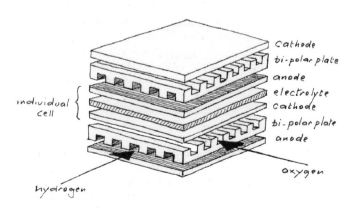

**Figure 7.3**   Fuel cell stack.

California was the pioneer in placing restrictions on fossil-fuel vehicles, requiring that 10% of cars in the state will be powered by hydrogen by 2004.

Italy has an accelerating problem of pollution from vehicles. The Lombardy region is particularly affected, with its capital Milan experiencing smog levels five times the legal limit. The result is that the regional government is considering a ban on the sales of all petrol and diesel cars after 2005.

It is unlikely that there will, in the near to medium term, be a network access to pure hydrogen for vehicles. In the interim it is most likely the gas will be catalysed from methanol.

## Phosphoric acid fuel cell (PAFC)

Similar to PEMFCs, this cell operates in the middle temperature range at around 200°C. This means it can tolerate some impurities. It employs a phosphoric acid proton conducting electrolyte and platinum or platinum–rhodium electrodes. The main difference from a PEMFC is that it uses a liquid electrolyte.

The system efficiency is currently in the 37–43% range, but this is expected to improve. This technology seems particularly popular in Japan where electricity costs are high and dispersed generation is preferred. A 200 kW unit which uses sewage gas provides heat and power for Yokohama sewage works. The largest installation to date for the Tokyo Electric Power Company had an output of 11 MW until it finally expired.

PAFC units have been used experimentally in buses. However, it is likely that its future lies in stationary systems.

The *New Scientist* editorial referred to above predicts that 'Larger, static fuel cells will become attractive for hotels and sports centres, while power companies will use them as alternatives to extending the electricity grid'. An example of this is the police station in Central Park, New York which found that installing a PAFC of 200 kW capacity was cheaper than a grid connection requiring new cables in the park. One year after this prediction the Borough of Woking, Surrey, installed the first commercial PAFC fuel cell to operate in the UK. It also has a capacity of 200 kW and will provide heat, cooling, light and dehumidification for the Pool in the Park recreation centre. The fuel cell will form part of Woking Park's larger combined heat and power system.

## Solid oxide fuel cell (SOFC)

This is a cell suitable only for static application, taking several hours to reach its operating temperature. It is a high temperature cell, running at between 800 and 1000°C. Its great virtue is that it can run on a range of fuels includ- ing natural gas and methanol which can be reformed within the cell. Its high operating temperature also enables it to break down impurities. Its high temperature also removes the need for noble metal catalysts such as platinum. Potentially, it has a wide range of power outputs from 2 to 1000 kW.

In contrast to PEMFCs, the electrolyte conducts oxygen ions rather than hydrogen ions that move from the cathode to the anode. The electrolyte is a ceramic which becomes conductive to oxygen ions at 800°C. SOFCs are often structured in a tubular rather than a planar form (as in the PEMFC) to reduce the chance of failure of the seals due to high temperature expansion. Air (oxygen) flows through a central tube while fuel flows round the outside of the structure (see Fig. 7.4).
According to David Hart:

> *Solid oxide fuel cells are expected to have the widest range of applications. Large units should be useful in industry for generating electricity and heat. Smaller units could be used in houses ...*[1]

There is confidence that the installed cost of static high temperature fuel cells will fall to $600–$1000 per kW. As cogeneration power units this will make them highly competitive with conventional systems. Already SOFCs are now being imported to the UK from the US at a cost of $1000 per kilowatt which is bringing them in range of cost effectiveness against fossil fuels.

At the time of writing Shell is considering SOFCs to power its oil and gas operations. However, its most likely future lies in providing combined heat and power either linked to buildings or housing estates or as providing direct grid support.

One of the main producers of SOFCs is Westinghouse, USA which uses the tubular configuration for the cell. A 200 kW unit has been installed on a test basis in The Netherlands.

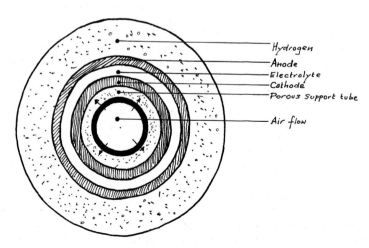

**Figure 7.4**  Solid oxide fuel cell in its tubular configuration.

## Alkaline fuel cell (AFC)

This fuel cell dates back to the 1940s and was the first to be fully developed in the 1960s. It was used in the Apollo spacecraft programme. It employs an alkaline electrolyte such as potassium hydroxide set between nickel or precious metal electrodes. Its operating temperature is 60–80°C which enables it to have a short warm-up time.

Its main drawback is that the electrolyte reacts with carbon dioxide which significantly reduces its performance. This means it has to use pure hydrogen and oxygen as its fuels. Another problem is that it has an energy density one-tenth that of PEMFCs which makes it much bulkier for a given output. On the plus side it is relatively cheap and has a role in static applications.

## Molten carbonate fuel cell (MCFC)

This is a high temperature fuel cell operating at about 650°C. The electrolyte in this case is an alkaline mixture of lithium and potassium carbonates which becomes liquid at 650°C and is supported by a ceramic matrix. The electrodes are both nickel based. The operation of the MCFC differs from that of other fuel cells in that it involves carbonate ion transfer across the electrolyte. This makes it tolerate both carbon monoxide and carbon dioxide. The cell can consume hydrocarbon fuels that are reformed into hydrogen within the cell.

The MCFC can achieve an efficiency of 55%. The steam and carbon dioxide it produces can be used to drive a turbine generator (cogeneration) which can raise the total efficiency to 80% – up to twice that of a typical oil- or gas-fired plant. Consequently this technology could be ideal for urban power stations producing combined heat and power. The Energy Research Corporation (ERC) of Danbury, Connecticut, USA has built a 2-MW unit for the municipality of Santa Clara, California and that company is currently developing a 2.85-MW plant.

Development programmes in Japan and the USA have produced small prototype units in the 5–20 kW range, which, if successful, will make them attractive for domestic combined heat and power.

The main disadvantage of the MCFC is that it uses as electrolytes highly corrosive molten salts that create both design and maintenance problems. Research is concentrating on solutions to these problems.

In March 2000 it was announced that researchers in the University of Pennsylvania in Philadelphia had developed a cell that could run directly off natural gas or methane. It did not have to be reformed to produce hydrogen. Other fuel cells cannot run directly on hydrocarbons which clog the catalyst within minutes. This innovative cell uses a copper and cerium oxide catalyst instead of nickel. The researchers consider that cars will be the main beneficiaries of the technology. However, Kevin Kendall, a chemist from the University of Keele, thinks differently. According to him 'Millions of homeowners replace their gas-fired central heating systems in Europe every year. Within five years they could be installing a fuel cell that would run on natural gas … Every home could have a combined heat and power plant running off mains gas'.[2]

International Fuel Cells (US) is testing a cell producing 5–10 kW of electricity and hot water at 120–160°C for heating. This is a residential system which it plans to have on the market by the end of 2002. The US company Plug Power which is linked to General Electric plans to market the 'GE HomeGen 7000' domestic fuel cell world-wide during 2002.

At the RIBA conference which triggered this book, Professor Tony Marmont offered a scenario whereby the fuel cell in a car would operate in conjunction with a home or office. He estimated that a car spends 96% of its time stationary so it would make sense to couple the car to a building to provide space heat and domestic hot water. The electricity generated amounting to about 50–80 kW would be sold to the grid. The car would be fuelled by a hydrogen grid. Until that is available, a catalyser within the car would reform methanol to provide the hydrogen. However, if the natural gas cell proves its worth, then it would simply draw its energy from the domestic supply.

Considerable research activity is focusing on fuel cells, particularly on how to reduce the costs of catalysts and improve energy density. One promising research programme is investigating how an enzyme substitute can break hydrogen molecules into their constituent atoms. The goal is a cheap catalyst which could transform the cost effectiveness of fuel cells. The principle is to mimic the hydrogenase enzyme adding ruthenium which performs most of the hydrogen-splitting operation. Ruthenium is up to 15 times cheaper than the conventional platinum.

The reason for the intensification of research activity is the belief that the fuel cell is the energy technology of the future in that it meets a cluster of needs, not least the fact that it can be a genuine zero carbon dioxide energy source. It could also relieve us of reliance on a national grid which, in many countries, is unreliable. Perhaps the greatest beneficiaries will be rural communities in developing countries who could never hope to get access to a grid supply. Access to energy is the main factor which divides the rich from the poor throughout the world. A cheap fuel cell powered by hydrogen electrolysed from PV, solar-electric or small-scale hydro-electricity could be the ultimate answer to this unacceptable inequality.

There is little doubt that we are approaching the threshold of the hydrogen-based economy. Ultimately hydrogen should be available 'on tap' through a piped network. In the meantime reforming natural gas, petrol, propane and other hydrocarbons to produce hydrogen would still result in massive reductions in carbon dioxide emissions and pollutants like oxides of sulphur and nitrogen. The domestic-scale fuel cells about to be marketed will have built-in processing units to reform hydrocarbon fuels and the whole system will occupy about the same space as a central heating boiler.

## Nuclear

Nuclear fusion is the ultimate reactor technology. For many decades it has been the pot of gold at the end of the energy rainbow. For most of the time it has been the province of high-energy physics. One favourite strategy has been to fuse two deuterium atoms: hydrogen with a neutron. The fusion of the two creates a massive surge of energy. The reaction can create hydrogen and radioactive tritium. The latter has a half-life of 12 years and can be turned into helium by fusing it with more deuterium. Compared with nuclear fission, it is a clean technology, producing minimal amounts of waste.

The stumbling block is that, in order to overcome the repulsive forces between the nuclei within the deuterium, the deuterium has to be heated to 10,000°C, the temperature at the heart of the sun. Maintaining the stability of matter at such a temperature is extremely difficult and consumes massive amounts of energy. As yet it has proved impossible to generate more energy from the process than is required to create the reaction. The theoretical belief is that ultimately fusion will create a net surplus of energy. For the past 50 years that goal has invariably been '50 years from now'. It still is.

This fact has led scientists to seek alternative routes to fusion. In 1989 scientists claimed to have achieved 'cold fusion' by electrolysing heavy water. No one was able to replicate the results. In 2002 an article in *Science* reported on an experiment which claimed to have achieved bench-top fusion.

For decades it has been known that sound waves in water can generate bubbles that heat to thousands of degrees as they collapse, emitting light in the process. The phenomenon is called 'sonoluminescence'. For fusion to occur the bubbles would have to reach nearly 10 million degrees. Researchers at Oakridge National Laboratory in Tennessee are not deterred by this challenge. Instead of water they have used acetone modified by replacing its hydrogen atoms with deuterium and chilling the liquid to 0°C. The acetone is bombarded with a neutron beam to produce tiny bubbles. Then sound waves cause the bubbles to expand before imploding. The neutrons released as deuterium fuse to form tritium, a result consistent with nuclear fusion. This result is being taken seriously, though commercial fusion is still a long way off; about 50 years.

## Notes

1. *New Scientist,* Inside Science, 'Fuelling the Future' 16 June 2001.
2. *New Scientist,* 18 March 2000.

# 8 Biogas

Up to the end of the nineteenth century a large proportion of commodities came from plant material. Even the first plastic invented in 1870, 'celluloid', was derived from cellulose extracted from cotton. By 1920, 70% of all energy consumed in the USA was supplied by coal. Finally, oil became the basis of the world's transportation systems.

Then came the oil shocks of the 1970s when the flow of oil to the west was severely curtailed. In 1969 the price of oil was 50 cents a barrel; by 1981 it had risen to $36. This galvanized the developed countries into action to find alternatives for oil, a process given further impetus by the Gulf War of the 1990s.

Advances in the biological sciences gave engineers the opportunity to raise the quality of industrial products derived from plants, while at the same time reducing their costs of production. In one case, the cost of industrial enzymes dropped 75% between 1975 and 1990.

The rise in the fortunes of the carbohydrate camp was given a considerable boost by the growing environmental awareness of the 1980s culminating in the Brundtland Commission and the international conference at Rio de Janiero. The outcome of this was the IPCC Report of 1992 which gave powerful scientific impetus to the phenomenon of global warming and the consequential climate changes. The report set out four scenarios for the future based on the extent to which countries would cut back on carbon dioxide and other greenhouse gas emissions. It was the first time that scientists had put a figure on the degree of abatement that would be needed to stabilize the atmosphere – 60% reduction world-wide against 1990 levels of emission.

A further factor in the equation was the environmental policies of developed nations which drove up the cost of waste disposal coupled with the banning of organic waste on waste sites. This stimulated the drive to find creative solutions to the problem of organic waste.

In terms of energy, many countries are looking to restructure their electricity industries in the face of powerful lobbies, for example in the US and UK, pressing for a de-centralized or distributed electricity system based on a range of renewable sources. Sweden and Germany are phasing out their nuclear capacity. The UK faces a serious energy shortfall when its nuclear and ageing coal-fired plants are decommissioned and will be faced with obtaining oil and gas from areas that are fraught with uncertainty (see Chapter 12).

All this has brought into sharper focus the need to exploit all renewable resources and one of the most abundant is biomass whether from energy crops or household waste. The technology to convert these into biogas together with farm and municipal sewage, offers an opportunity to answer several pressing problems simultaneously.

## Biogas from anaerobic digestion

This is a process which converts biomass, such as rapid-rotation crops and selected domestic and farm waste including slurry and sewage sludge, to a gas that can fuel a gas turbine, an internal combustion engine or a Stirling engine. Gasification has a number of advantages:

- a relatively high efficiency for electricity production at a considerable range of scales
- lends itself to combined heat and power application
- creates low to almost zero carbon dioxide emissions depending on the fuel and because of the small gas flow compared with traditional fossil-fuel generation
- virtually eliminates noxious odours and methane and nitrous oxide emissions
- reduces the landfill burden
- protects ground water
- supports the Kyoto Protocol on reducing greenhouse gases.

It is a technology that is still undergoing research to improve the gasification process and its adaptability to a range of fuels.

Anaerobic digestion produces biogas by the conversion of organic substances through microbiological processes that occur in the absence of oxygen. The constituents of the gas are 50–70% methane, 27–43% carbon dioxide plus small amounts of nitrogen and trace impurities. It has considerable potential as a component of a country's energy mix. For example, Germany could meet 11% of its current gas consumption from this source. In that country it is estimated that over 220,000 farm-based and centralized biogas plants could operate purely on farm waste.

Of considerable potential benefit is the fact that biogas, after some purification, can be used to produce reformed hydrogen for fuel cells. Most suitable would be high temperature fuel cells like molten carbonate and solid oxide versions operating at 800–1000°C. For phosphoric acid and proton exchange membrane fuel cells further purification would be needed.

An initial estimate is that the potential in the UK is for over 200 anaerobic digestion plants either for the codigestion of farm slurry/sewage sludge and food waste or household waste on its own. In addition there is almost unlimited potential for biomass plants using coppicing of rapid rotation crops like willow in set-aside land.

## Biogas from farm slurry

The first plant in the UK to use farm manure and food waste began operation in March 2002. It is situated in Holsworthy, Devon and was built by a German company using a technology familiar in that country. The operating company Holsworthy Biogas expects to process 146,000 tonnes a year of cattle, pig and poultry manure from up to 30 local farms within a radius of 10 miles.

### The process

Manure and food waste are discharged into a reception tank and during unloading air is passed through a biofilter to reduce noxious smells. The waste is then discharged into another mixing tank where the mixture is heated to 70°C. This is the pasteurization process which lasts an hour and serves to kill all pathogens, viruses and weed seeds.

After pasteurization the mix is pumped through a heat exchanger into a digester chamber where anaerobic digestion takes place at 37°C for a period of about 20 days. The end product is a methane-rich gas which is cleaned in a de-sulphurization unit prior to being stored in a tank.

The residue of the process called the digestate is a high-quality bio-fertilizer that is returned to the farmers in lorries that are designed to carry the fertilizer and return with the farm slurry.

The plant's annual gas production is estimated to be 3.9 million m$^3$ equivalent to 39 million kWh per year. The gas is used to heat two gas engines with a total power output of approximately 2.1 MW and the electricity will be sold to the grid. The excess heat is expected to be used for a new district heating scheme planned for the end of 2002.

## Gasification from biomass

In this case a methane-rich gas is produced from biomass such as coppiced wood from rapid rotation crops such as willow. Because the growing process takes up carbon from the atmosphere and then returns it when it is burned, the process is said to be carbon neutral. This is disputed by the Institute of Chemical Engineers which states, in a response to a government

**Figure 8.1**   Eggborough gasification plant.

consultation paper, that 'energy crops should not be considered carbon dioxide neutral. The growing period requires energy which is not always recovered and this affects the overall balance in $CO_2$.'[1]

However, the process could be said to be 'virtually' carbon dioxide neutral.

Known as the ARBRE project (Arable Biomass Renewable Energy) the first biomass to biogas plant at Eggborough in the UK began full operation in 2001. As a joint UK–Swedish project it was designed with the twin objectives of:

- establishing dedicated short-rotation energy crops as a viable energy source
- constructing a high efficiency combined cycle power station supplied by this fuel (see Fig. 8.1).

Designed to achieve an output of 10 MW, sufficient to provide domestic electricity for 35,000 people, the plant uses atmospheric gasification to convert woody biomass into electricity. It employs what is called the atmospheric circulating fluidized bed (CFB) process that enjoys the further complicated title of an Integrated Gasification Combined Cycle (IGCC) system. As such it claims high efficiency and low emissions from combustion.

The gasification CFB system offers significantly higher efficiency and reduced emissions compared with a straight combustion plant.

## The process

Wood in chip form is fed into a fuel reception building where it is dried by the flue gas from a waste heat boiler. Then the dried chipped wood and process air are fed continuously into the lower part of the gasification chamber which contains a sand bed. Air entering the bottom of the vessel serves to 'fluidize' sand and fuel.

This is the first stage in forming a combustible gas, which, on leaving the gasifier, contains ash, wood char and sand all of which are separated out by means of 'cyclones' and returned to the base of the gasifier.

The raw gas passes to a 'tar cracker' which serves to break down the heavy hydrocarbons. The gas leaving the cracker consists of methane, hydrogen, carbon dioxide and nitrogen together with water vapour and trace levels of heavy hydrocarbons.

The gas is then cooled and any residual dust collected in bag filters. After a further cooling phase the gas passes to a wet scrubber to remove water vapour and ammonia plus any other traces of alkali compounds and hydrocarbons.

In this particular plant the gas leaving the scrubber is split into two routes. The main stream is compressed and powers a gas turbine coupled to an electricity generator. The secondary stream goes to heat a boiler designed to use gas with a relatively low calorific value. Flue gas leaving the gas turbine provides additional heating for the boiler which produces superheated steam to power a steam turbine. It is the combination of the two generators which provides the 10 MW of electricity to the grid.

As agricultural policy within the European Union is clamping down on excess arable and livestock production, more and more land is becoming available encouraging farmers to diversify into rapid rotation crop development. The exploitation of this 'set-aside' land could form a major element in the post-fossil-fuel energy regime which is inevitably the shape of the future (see Fig. 8.2).

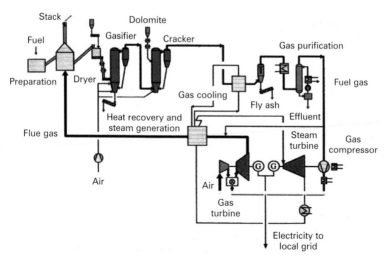

**Figure 8.2** ARBRE biogas system, Eggborough.

## Biogas from municipal waste

### *The Kongsberg project*

This is a town in Buskerud county of Norway. It produced 21,000 m³/year of raw sludge. Because of legislation concerning landfill waste the municipality decided to invest in a pilot anaerobic digestion plant designed to process 2500 tonnes per year of wet organic waste together with raw sewage sludge. In this process organic waste is deposited in a closed and ventilated building. It is then transported to a mixer where solid, hard objects like stones and metal are removed. This incoming waste is then heated and fed to the digestion vessel or biogas reactor. After the anaerobic digestion by microbial action is complete the gas powers a CHP plant generating 1.3 GWh/year of electricity and 1.9 GWh/year of heat. The treated sludge is marketed as a fertilizer.

Every community is faced with the prospect of an ever-increasing problem of waste disposal, in particular the environmentally benign disposal of sewage. The town of Hamar in Norway has built a plant to process sewage sludge from a population of 10,000. It began operation in 1995, processing about 57 tonnes per day of sludge and supplying net energy of 15,000 kWh/day in the form of superheated steam at 10-bar pressure. The process includes a stage called 'thermal hydrolysis' namely a chemical breakdown of the material due to a reaction with water and heat at high pressure. The process leads to the conversion of complex organic material like proteins, lipids and cellulose fibres into simpler chemical substances more amenable to digestion.

The process results in several marketable products. The dried residual sludge is ideal as a cover for landfill and recultivation sites. The nitrogen in the sludge can be converted to a fertilizer. The plant is designed to utilize a gas engine for supplying electricity to the grid.

While all this is not 'cutting-edge' technology it is likely that anaerobic digestion of municipal and agricultural slurry and household waste will become established as a significant component in the strategy to realize a sustainable future source of energy often with the side benefit of high-grade fertilizer.

From the point of view of carbon dioxide emissions the most effective use of biogas is to power a fuel cell. Because of their similar composition biogas can be a substitute for natural gas. The only drawback is that biogas has a lower calorific value due to the presence of carbon dioxide. After some purification it can be used for high-temperature fuel cells such as a molten carbonate fuel cell and a solid oxide fuel cell operating at 800–1000°C.

As stated earlier, the biogas that emerges from anaerobic digestion contains about 60% methane, 37% carbon dioxide and 2% hydrogen sulphide. The first stage in the purification process involves the removal of sulphur by absorption on ferrous oxide and charcoal. Then halogen is removed again by charcoal. The next stage sees the removal of siloxane by cooling to −2°C plus absorption on charcoal. Finally moisture and solids are removed making it suitable for high temperature fuel cells. Additional purification is required for phosphoric acid and proton exchange membrane fuel cells since their lower operating temperature does not burn off impurities. This means higher capital and operating costs than with high-temperature fuel cells. Another advantage of the latter is that they are about 8% more efficient than PAFCs and PEMFCs.

An experimental project in Germany involving the anaerobic digestion of organic household and restaurant waste is due to begin operation in mid-2002. It has a capacity of 18,000 tonnes per year which produces 1.3 million $m^3$ of raw biogas equivalent to 10 million kWh. This gas will be processed to a level suitable for a high temperature fuel cell. Initially it will power gas engines but the proposal is to replace one of the engines with a high temperature fuel cell. Despite high initial costs, under the renewable energy legislation, the electricity delivered to the grid will produce a substantial bonus.

Including the German project, at present there are only four biogas to fuel cell operations in the world with all four based on PAFC technology. Two are in the US, one in Germany operating on sewage gas and one in Chiba, Japan. The last at Chiba Brewery uses biogas extracted from the plant's organic waste water. The brewery effluent is supplemented by waste from food companies in the same business park. Conventional treatment costs for the waste from the brewery are high, therefore the alternative of anaerobic digestion to form biogas was an attractive alternative. The company elected to install a 200 kW phosphoric acid fuel cell that can use 80% of the energy content of the biogas as electricity and heat. The total output of the system is 200 kWe (electricity) and 205 kWth (heat). It is generating 1728 MWh per year of electricity and 1768 MWh per year of heat. The operation is saving the company ¥30 million per year.[2]

In conclusion, two technologies can be used to process separated organic waste. A team from the Netherlands has compared the performance of two plants, one using anaerobic digestion, the other, composting in aerobic conditions. The composting process takes 6–11 weeks. The result was that the anaerobic plant achieved greater reductions in carbon dioxide and produced biogas for the production of energy. Despite consuming more than four times as much primary energy as the composting plant, the anaerobic plant is a net energy producer.

The medium- to long-term outlook seems to favour anaerobic digestion of waste, including municipal and agricultural sewage, coupled to a high temperature fuel cell. This is a technology that offers a cluster of virtuous circles.

## Notes

1. *The Chemical Engineer*, p. 24, 23 September 1999.
2. Caddet, *Renewable Energy Newsletter*, July 1999.

# 9  Micro-power

It has already been suggested that there is an increasing trend towards 'distributed' or decentralized power generation, especially in rural locations or where stability of supply is essential, such as for banks, hospitals research facilities and so on. Micro-power or small-scale generation is the key to this trend. There are several advantages to this alternative to the large-scale grid system served by a few large thermal power plants:

- Small-scale power can be closer to the point of use, overcoming the inefficiency of long distribution lines.
- It can be scaled to meet the exact requirements of the consumer. For example, in the US domestic consumers use an average rate of 1.5 kW.
- In most of its versions it has a relatively high efficiency by producing both electricity and heat.
- There are considerable environmental cost-avoidance benefits.
- In some cases it is modular, meaning that it can be scaled up or down to meet changing needs.
- Small-scale power has a short lead time and can be planned, built and commissioned in a much shorter time than is the case with larger plants.
- It can obviate the need for new large-scale power plants often subject to public enquiry. This is especially important in the case of new nuclear installations.
- Micro-power is capable of running on a variety of fuels emitting rates of particulates, sulphur dioxide, nitrogen oxides and carbon dioxide that are significantly lower than larger plants. In the case of direct hydrogen, this means zero emissions.
- It is largely immune to the price volatility of fossil fuels distributed by the large utilities, a fact that will be increasingly advantageous as oil and gas prices reflect diminishing reserves or political tensions.

- There can be community control and choice of the technology. This can trigger local initiatives like a plant for the treatment of sewage through anaerobic digestion to produce biogas for the energy system.

The shift to distributed or embedded generation is part of a trend which was first witnessed in computers. Mainframe and mini-computers were all but vanquished by the personal computer, just as the fixed telephone has been severely challenged by the mobile phone and e-mail.

The virtue of a distributed system is endorsed by the Washington World-watch Institute which states:

*An electricity grid with many small generators is inherently more stable than a grid serviced by only a few large plants. So-called intelligent grids which can receive as well as distribute electricity at every node are already emerging.*

## Market predictions for micro-power

A study published in July 1999 by the US Business Communications Company estimates that small-scale power will account for a significant portion of the predicted 200 GW of new capacity expected world-wide by 2003. In the US the market is anticipated to grow at an annual rate of 32% over the next several years.

The installed value of fuel cells is expected to grow from $305 million in 1998 to $1.1 billion by 2003.

Micro-turbines were almost zero in 1998 and are set to reach $8.1 billion by 2003 – almost half the total US small-scale capacity.

By 2010 the installed value of fuel cells powered from renewable sources should reach at least $10 billion.

Seth Dunn of the Washington Worldwatch Institute believes that micro-power is the shape of the future for energy:

*It is not inconceivable that, in the long run, most of society's power will come from small scale local systems, with the rest coming from large wind farms and solar plants making centralized thermal plants no longer necessary.*[1]

## Micro-turbines

This is the technology which looks set to penetrate the US market at a phenomenal rate. Micro-turbines are a spin-off from the jet-engine industry. Heat released by combustion at high speed drives turbine blades that, in turn, spin a high-speed generator. Their power output ranges from 15 to 300 kW. If their waste heat is usefully employed they are highly efficient.

Having only two moving parts they are straightforward to manufacture and consequently relatively cheap. Maintenance is kept to a minimum since no lubricants or coolants are required. Their life expectancy is about 40,000 hours.

Another benefit is that turbines can use a variety of fuels, for example, natural gas, propane, kerosene, diesel fuel and biogas. The last is of particular interest since anaerobic digestion processing of biological waste to produce biogas may become increasingly popular.

It is a technology that is specially suitable for the domestic and small business market. Groups of homes needing between 25 and 300 kW of power will be obvious candidates for micro-turbines, especially with their CHP/cogeneration potential.

The US producer of micro-turbines, Capstone, predicts that this will be a $1 billion industry within 5 years. Assuming the economy of scale of at least 100,000 units per year, a 30 kW turbine would cost $400/kW. Ultimately a 100 kW unit could cost as little as $200/kW which is less than half that of the most economic conventional power plants.

## Stirling engines

It is interesting how two nineteenth-century technologies, the fuel cell and the Stirling engine, are only now coming into their own. Invented by Robert Stirling in 1816, the engine that bears his name is described as an 'external combustion engine'. Because of advances in piston technology and in materials like ceramics from the space industry and high temperature steels allowing temperatures to rise to 1200°C, it is now considered a firm contender for the micro-power market.

The operational principle is that a fixed amount of gas is sealed within the engine. In present-day engines this is helium. It works on the basis that when the temperature of a specific amount of gas within a fixed volume of space is raised the pressure will increase. At the same time, compressing the gas within the fixed volume will raise its temperature. Heat is applied to the exterior of the engine to achieve this change of state of a gas.

A basic Stirling engine has two cylinders. One is heated by the external source while the other is cooled by an external sink that can include the surrounding air. The two cylinders are connected and contain pistons which are mechanically linked in such a way as to optimize the power potential of the heating and cooling of the gas. There are four phases to the engine's cycle.

During the first phase of the cycle, heat is applied to the left cylinder causing pressure to increase, pushing the piston down. This is the work phase of the cycle.

The right piston is at the top of its travel to maximize the pressure (see Fig. 9.1).

For the second phase, after completing its downward travel the left piston moves up while the downward track of the right cylinder draws hot gas into the right chamber where it is cooled, thus losing pressure.

On its third stroke the right piston moves upwards compressing the gas while cold.

The final stroke sees the right piston move to the top of its travel while the left moves down drawing cold gas into the left chamber to be heated.

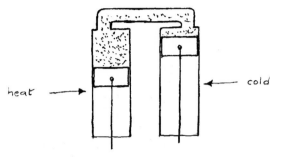

**Figure 9.1** Basic two-cylinder Stirling external combustion engine.

An alternative design is the 'displacer' type of engine. In this case there is only one tight fitting piston within a cylinder above a larger cylinder containing a displacer. This is a loose fitting piston that allows gas to flow between the upper and lower parts of the chamber. The bottom of the chamber is continually heated and the top cooled. Again the two pistons are linked so that the sealed piston reaches the bottom of its travel to coincide with the displacer piston reaching the top of its journey. This is the work stage as the smaller piston is forced upwards. As the displacer piston moves down the gas is forced into the cooler part of the cylinder causing it to contract. This lowers the pressure allowing the small piston to move down and compress the gas ready for the power cycle. At the same time, the upward movement of the displacer then forces cooled gas into the lower chamber to be heated and made to expand and so the engine repeatedly heats and cools the gas extracting energy from expansion and contraction (see Fig. 9.2).

A third variation on the Stirling theme is a two-cylinder engine with the cylinders set at 90° to each other. The horizontal cylinder is heated while the vertical is air cooled. In the first phase heated gas expands forc-

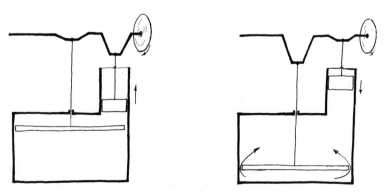

**Figure 9.2** Two phases of the displacer Stirling engine.

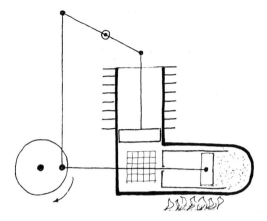

**Figure 9.3** Stirling engine 90° opposed version.

ing the horizontal cylinder to move to the left. This is the power stroke (see Fig. 9.3).

In the next phase the heated piston moves to the right while the cool piston moves upwards. This causes the gas to migrate to the cool cylinder via what is termed a regenerative unit. This is a device which captures some of the heat from the gas as it is expelled from the heated cylinder in order to pre-heat gas returning to the power cylinder.

Finally the cool piston moves down forcing the gas through the regenerative unit and the cycle recommences.

The Stirling engine offers several benefits:

• It can use any combustible fuel from agricultural and forestry waste to biogas and natural gas.
• It is relatively efficient especially when used for CHP.
• It is robust, being of simple construction and requiring low maintenance.
• It is quiet running which makes it suitable for domestic application.
• It is durable, offering up to 60,000 hours of life.
• It is moderately priced.

### Commercial applications

In the UK the Stirling technology is being developed for the market by BG Technology, the research arm of British Gas. It is now testing a 1.1 kW CHP system that runs on natural gas and is being aimed at the domestic market.

In the coming decade it is likely that the Stirling engine will play a significant part in the shift to combined heat and power in the domestic sector. This is because it is the only CHP unit presently available which can be scaled down to suit an individual house. The so-called 'personal CHP' can be wall mounted to produce 15 kW of heat as well as electricity. It only supplies electricity whilst there is a demand for heat which means that its main electricity production is during the colder months. Any shortfall in demand is met by the grid.

According to the BG Group the estimated average cost saving in electricity is £200 per year at present prices. Surplus electricity can be directed to the grid, though it must be said that the current bureaucratic minefield protecting the interests of the utilities will have to be cleared before supplying the grid from a small plant becomes attractive. A first priority is for the buy-in price per kilowatt paid by the utilities to at least equal the price they charge the consumer. The situation should be regularized when the whole of the European Union has to liberalize its electricity market by 2010.

According to an EA Technology report, Stirling CHP will reduce the energy bill of the average household by 20%, and that is without taking account of sales to the grid. Also, if every one of the 13 million homes in Britain suited to Stirling CHP installed the technology it would reduce UK carbon emissions by 16 million tonnes per year. That would amount to 61% of the UK's carbon abatement commitment under the Kyoto Protocol. Add to this the potential for energy savings due to improved insulation across the housing stock and homes could almost do it alone.

The compact Stirling engine used in this capacity is of the piston and displacer type. Heat is applied to the top of the unit with a heat sink at the base. The heat flow from top to bottom produces the difference in temperature and thus the fluctuation in pressure which powers the piston. The cool end of the unit provides thermal energy for heating water. If flue gases can be passed through a heat exchanger this would optimize system efficiency. As stated in Chapter 4, even greater gains can be realized when the system is coupled to a ground or water source heat pump.

In the US the External Power Company has produced a biomass-fuelled 1 kW Stirling engine providing heat and power at the domestic scale. This is a package which recovers significant amounts of heat from the exhaust gases which is transferred to the incoming combustion gases to increase overall efficiency. The first prototypes are fuelled by wood pellets. There are plans to scale up the output to 20 kW for larger residential and commercial application.

This technology is ideal for the domestic market, being quiet, low maintenance and economical. Ultimately it may be supplanted by the single house fuel cell, but that is unlikely for perhaps a couple of decades.

A hybrid system has been developed by the STM Corporation of the US which marries a solar collector to a Stirling engine. The solar collector or 'SunDish' consists of an array of mirrors which tracks the path of the sun focusing its rays on a thermal concentrator. The solar energy is focused onto a hemispherical absorber in the engine's heat pipe receiver. The heat pipe receiver transfers heat at between 300 and 800°C to the Stirling engine which is hermetically sealed producing daytime electricity with zero emissions. At night the engine is heated by a range of possible fuels including landfill gas, wood chippings and biogas from an anaerobic digester. An operating cost of about 3.2 cents per kWh is claimed (see Fig. 2.17).

This is a promising technology particularly for 'solar-rich' developing countries. Its makers claim that their SunDish technology can produce up to 250 MW of power. As they say, 'The only limit is the land'.

## Note

1. Quoted in *Renewable Energy World* November–December, 2000.

# 10  Small-scale hydro

Hydro-power has a history going back at least 2000 years. The Doomsday book records 5000 waterwheels. One of the earliest hydroelectric schemes and first in the world to power a private home was installed by the First Lord Armstrong in the 1880s at Cragside in Northumberland. This means, of course, that it is not exactly at the cutting edge of progress. The expansion of the National Grid sounded the death knell for many small-hydro schemes. However, it is increasingly now being perceived as an important source of clean electricity, devoid of the environmental penalties associated with large scale hydro-power. It has minimal impact on the environment resulting in almost zero emissions of sulphur dioxide, carbon dioxide and nitrous oxides. Nor does it cause acidification of water; on the contrary it can oxygenate rivers and streams.

A life-cycle comparison with coal and combined cycle natural gas makes the point (see Table 10.1).

**Table 10.1** Life-cycle emissions (g/kW h)

|  | $CO_2$ | $SO_2$ | $NO_x$ |
|---|---|---|---|
| Small-hydro | 3.6–11.6 | 0.009–0.024 | 0.003–0.006 |
| Natural gas combined cycle | 402 | 0.2 | 0.3 |
| Coal | 1026 | 1.2 | 1.8 |

Renewable energy systems have 31 times less impact on the environment than fossil-based energy, with 1 kWh produced by small-scale hydro being 300 times less polluting than the dirtiest of them all, lignite.

Another method of comparison is to award ecopoints to the various technologies. These are points of environmental penalty. The factors considered include global warming, ozone depletion, acidification, eutrophication of water, heavy-metal pollution, emission of carcinogens, production of winter and summer smog, industrial waste, radioactive waste and radioactivity and depletion of energy resources.

Table 10.2 compares small-hydro with other energy sources on this basis.

**Table 10.2**

| Fuel | Ecopoints |
|---|---|
| Fuel oil | 1398 |
| Coal | 1356 |
| Nuclear | 672 |
| Natural gas | 267 |
| Small-hydro | 5 |

Source: APPA (Spain) Study on Environmental Impact of the Production of Electricity.

According to a European Union White Paper *A Community Strategy and Action Plan for the Future: Renewable Sources of Energy* (1997) 'only about 20% of the economic potential for small-hydro power plants has so far been exploited … An additional installed capacity of 4500 MW of small-hydro plants by 2010 is a realistic contribution which could be achieved'. The Community guidelines also recognize the need to internalize the external costs of electricity generation. Investments in renewables are deemed to be equivalent to environmental investments.

Having said all this, there is a sting in the tail. The European Commission does *not* consider that small-hydro should receive support as a source of renewable energy. This is because it reckons that large-scale hydro can produce electricity at market prices. Small-hydro suffers because of this blanket perception. It also reveals that the Commission is still driven by market rather than environmental considerations since small-hydro is one of the cleanest of all technologies as stated above.

As for defining small-hydro the European Union regards 10 MW as the demarcation line. There are two ways of extracting energy from situations capable of providing a head of water. They both depend on geographical/geological characteristics and the location of a suitable water source:

• Mountainous country provides a high hydraulic head of water that makes a high-speed impulse turbine the appropriate conversion technology.
• River valleys usually only create opportunities for a low head of water, generally less than 20 m. In this case water is diverted to a pipe (penstock) or channel (leat) leading to a crossflow turbine like an updated water wheel or a Kaplan turbine which has variable blades. Turbines are now available which can exploit as little as 2–3 m head of water.

The essential components of a hydro-scheme are:

• an adequate rainfall catchment area
• a weir or dam to provide a suitable head of water

- alternatively a river with a suitable drop in level to enable water to be diverted to a penstock or leat to be delivered to a turbine at the right speed and in the right quantity
- a turbine, generator and electrical connection
- a tailrace to return water to the river.

One of the concerns about this technology is that it can deplete fish stocks. Some reports implicate small-hydro in the destruction of salmon fishing in a part of Spain. The remedy is a fish channel suitable for even the smallest fish incorporating an acoustic guidance system to prevent fish entering the forebay of the plant. An alternative is an electric fish screen which was first tested at a 500 kW installation at Deanston, Scotland.

In the UK the most abundant small-hydro potential is in Scotland. An example of a community initiative to harness small-hydro energy is the 230 kW scheme at Lock Poll within the North Assynt Estate in Sutherland. The Assynt Crofters' Trust constructed a dam to raise the level of the Lock. Water channelled along a penstock drives a turbine driven generator which produces around 1.32 GWh of electricity per year. The Trust has a 15-year contract to sell to the grid. This is the most northerly hydroelectric project in the UK and has been the basis of a study into the provision of small-hydro serving remote communities.

A 200 kW turbine is currently under construction at a weir on the River Thames. This location is important since it will raise the profile of small-hydro within the metropolitan field of influence.

How discrete small-hydro can be within an area of outstanding beauty such as the Snowdonia National Park is illustrated by the Garnedd power station near Dolwyddelan, north Wales. It is a run-of-river scheme which taps the energy from the Tyn-y-ddol river. Water is fed into a penstock pipe from a small pond 1 km from the plant and with a static head of 102 m. A Turgo impulse turbine drives a synchronous generator producing up to 600 kW and an average of 2.3 GW/h per year. The power station is operated and monitored remotely.

Similarly discreet is the small-hydro plant at Tanygrisiau which discharges its tail race into the lake which serves the pump storage Ffestiniog power station (see Fig. 10.1).

One of the most cost-effective ways of installing small-hydro is to restore the infrastructure created for industrial water power, usually in eighteenth or nineteenth century mills.

A successful run-of-river low-head project has been in operation at Blantyre Mill on the River Clyde since 1995. With an output of 576 kW it supplies the grid under contract. The site has a 200-year tradition of exploiting water power for a cotton mill later to become a sawmill. Salmon have been returning to the Clyde and so a by-pass channel for the fish is incorporated into the scheme.

Occasionally older hydro power plants have been abandoned as grid delivered power became economically attractive. Now things have gone full

**Figure 10.1**   Ffestiniog small-hydro plant, Tanygrisiau, north Wales.

circle and hydro installations are being refurbished. An example is the East Mill in Belper, Derbyshire, a low head run-of-river scheme linked to a weir.

## Micro-hydro and developing countries

Despite often having access to wind or hydro-power, about two billion people or one-third of the earth's population have no electricity. Many small communities, especially in the developing world, do not have the resources to embark on a small-hydro project, but *micro-hydro* is another matter. It covers systems providing between 10 and 100 kW of power. A typical case is the Vavanga Community, a village on the south-west coast of Kolombangara Island, one of the Solomon Islands. It now has electricity thanks to Appropriate Technology for Community and Environment (APACE) based in NSW Australia, a non-profit community-based agency assisting overseas communities to engage in sustainable development.

The system consists of a timber weir feeding a four-pipe penstock which powers a turbine serving a 240 V AC synchronous generator with an output of 4–7 kW, depending on the season. The power is fed to the village 2 km away by a combination of underground and overhead cable. In the first instance 22 houses, 14 kitchens, two church premises and a bakery were connected to the supply. Typically two 18 W fluorescent lights and one power point are served in each household. To ensure that the river can supply an equitable amount of power when rates of flow vary, a current limiting device is installed in each household. However, community facilities and businesses receive unlimited power.

Villagers took an active part in the installation of the project. As a run-of-river scheme it is mechanically relatively straightforward which has

**Figure 10.2**  Villagers of Vavanga maintaining the plant. (Courtesy of Caddet.)

enabled the villagers to be trained to carry out routine maintenance (see Fig. 10.2). Oversight is provided by APACE which liaises with the community hydro committee regarding local resource utilization, local distribution and the design of buildings.

The electrification of Vavanga and similar villages has a variety of positive impacts, not least the fact that it has slowed the population migration from villages to towns. There is now better village welfare. New homes are being built connected to the supply. There is a new church. Existing homes are being repaired and well maintained. There is street lighting.

The community plans to upgrade the system, first by replacing the timber weir with a concrete structure and second, to tap an additional tributary of the river with a second penstock feeding a small turbine.

The cause of micro-hydro has recently been further advanced by the development of a 'power controller' by a Danish engineer, Steen Carlsen. This makes it possible to create stand-alone power plants much more cheaply. It supplies AC current to a quality matching that from a large public grid and at a price that is a mere fraction of that from traditional synchronous generators previously necessary for stand-alone plants. The device provides a fixed voltage within a margin of 1%. This has an impact on the life of light bulbs for example. If a filament bulb receives an excess voltage of 10% its life expectancy is reduced by 70%. In developing countries this is an important consideration. Another problem with isolated off-grid communities is that they have a problem with surplus electricity.

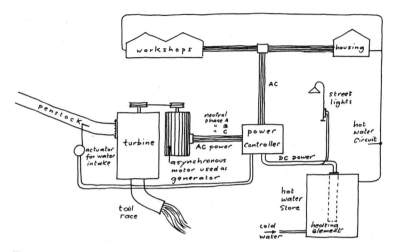

**Figure 10.3**  Typical village system with power controller.

A village in the Peruvian Andes was the first to receive the power controller. The device maintains a steady three-phase output from a turbine driven asynchronous motor by diverting surplus power to a heating cartridge (a large immersion heater) in a central tank which can distribute hot water to the community (see Fig. 10.3).

A further trick of the power controller is that it can 'deceive' conventional electric motors into acting as though they were connected to the grid. This allows cheap standard electric motors to be used as generators, enabling wind or hydro-schemes to operate in either stand-alone or grid connected mode.

The fact that the inhabitants can now heat their homes and domestic water from the micro-hydro source has meant that they are no longer reliant on wood from the surrounding forests. So, it is countering 'survival' deforestation and the erosion of soil which accompanies it. It is also providing power for small-scale industries and workshops, further placing a brake on the drift to the cities.

Finally, a Yorkshire farmer, Bill Cowperthwaite, has demonstrated how micro-hydro can come within the do-it-yourself range. His ideas have been adopted by the charity Intermediate Technology. The principle is to use components which are cheap and readily available in developing countries. What is required is a length of metal or PVC pipe for the penstock, a standard pump, and an electric motor. The pump is converted into a turbine by reversing the connections. If pumps are not available Intermediate Technology has devised a programme for teaching villagers how to fabricate turbines from waste metal. The electric motor can be converted into a generator. Electric motors work by generating an electric field within the motor which causes a magnet at the core of the motor to spin. Generators work in reverse

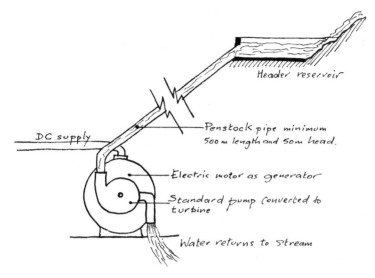

**Figure 10.4**   Improvised micro-hydro with converted electric motor as generator.

by spinning the central magnet causing current to flow to the external electromagnet. Capacitors are all that are required to convert the motors into generators. These store electricity for the short time required to even out the variations in voltage as the core rotates. It is reckoned that the cost of an electric motor and converting it to work as a generator is significantly less than the cost of a purpose-built generators for rating up to 20 kW. There is a bonus in that electric motors generally have heavier bearings than commercial generators giving them a life expectancy of at least 10 years (see Fig. 10.4).

The final piece of the kit is an electric controller which manages the flow of electricity. As in the Peruvian scheme the controller directs electricity which is temporarily surplus to demand to a heat sink. The controllers can be made locally and are already being manufactured in numerous rural sites for example in Nepal.

Whilst small-hydro has considerable potential in the industrialized countries, micro-hydro in association with other compact renewable technologies raises the possibility of transforming the lives of rural communities in developing countries.

# 11 Wave and tide

Maritime nations have a huge energy resource in the form of waves. In *Architecture in a Climate of Change*[1] a number of emerging wave technologies were described. This chapter explores further systems which are at or near the development stage. The sea is, in effect, a huge mass–spring system which oscillates with a fixed frequency. The average wave length is around 120 m and, in high seas, a wave carries about 100 kW/m of potential energy.

## Point absorbers

As the term suggests, these are systems which are focused on a nodal form of absorbing the energy of the waves to generate electricity. One technology which is on the verge of being market ready is the Interproject Service (IPS) Offshore Wave Energy Converter (OWEC) system. This uses only wave energy and is not affected by tidal or ocean currents.

The system consists of a floating buoy (A) attached to the seabed by 'elastic' moorings enabling it to exploit the motion of the waves. The buoy height is 5–6 m with a diameter of 5–10 m and requires a water depth of 40–50 m. Attached to the buoy is a vertical tube or 'acceleration tube' (B) of a length around three times the diameter of the buoy up to 25 m. Within the acceleration tube there is a free-moving piston (C) which has a restricted stroke to prevent overloading of the system (see Fig. 11.1).

The principle is that the buoy moves vertically against the damping mass of the water in the acceleration tube under the buoy. The relative movement between the buoy and the water mass in the tube is transferred by the piston (D) into the energy conversion system consisting of a hydraulic pumping cylinder which, via a hydraulic motor, drives the generator (E).

The OWEC converts 30–35% of the energy of the waves into electricity. It is suggested that there would be clusters of units making up a complete power plant which could generate over 200 kW.

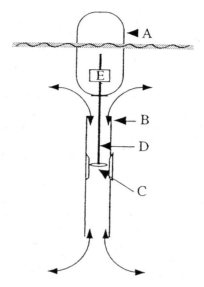

**Figure 11.1**   IPS OWEC wave generator Courtesy of Interproject Service AB.

The Danish Maritime Institute has developed another form of point absorber which also employs a float connected by a polyester rope to a suction cup anchor. The rope is attached to a hydraulic actuator within the float that pumps fluid into a high-pressure hydraulic accumulator. The return stroke is provided by a hydraulic fluid from a low-pressure accumulator. As waves create motion in the float, a pressure difference between the high and low pressure accumulators builds up. The pressure difference drives a hydraulic motor and generator. A system with a 5–6 m diameter would have a rated output of 20–30 kW. The ultimate objective is to construct a 10 m buoy with an output of around 120 kW (see Fig. 11.2).

A variation on the theme has been developed by the Energy Centre of the Netherlands (ECN). It is called the Archimedes Wave Swing and consists of a number of air-filled chambers below the surface of the sea. Above these are movable floats in the form of hoods which oscillate vertically with the pressure created by the wave motion. These would be about 20 m in diameter and weigh roughly 1000 tonnes. The top of each float is shaped like a funnel that maximizes the point absorbing effect. As a wave crest moves over the hood, the internal pressure rises. The trapped air is pushed into another chamber and the hood begins its descent. The process is reversed in a wave trough. The vertical motion is converted to rotary action to drive a generator. The system is positioned about 20 m below the surface with the float designed to be in balance with that amount of water above it. At this depth the system is protected from damage from extreme storms (see Fig. 11.3).

The intention is that groups of three floats will be connected so that as a wave progresses it create a succession of oscillations. It is reckoned that a three chamber unit will produce about 2.7 MW.

## Wave absorbers

The Danish Wave Energy Programme which was started in 1998 has produced several concepts for the exploitation of wave energy. The aim is to examine the feasibility of plants that can be up to gigawatt scale thereby providing 15% of Denmark's electricity.

First there is the 'Wave Dragon' which comprises a floating power plant in deep water. The waves are captured by a platform between two concrete reflectors 227 m apart. These focus the waves into a 2600 m$^3$ floating reservoir. From the reservoir the water flows back into the sea via turbines at a rate of 100 m$^3$/s. This is still at the experimental stage awaiting the verdict on the performance of a 1:3 scale version (see Fig. 11.4).

An idea which originated in Japan and developed in China, elegantly titled 'Backward Bend Duct Buoy', consists of a float carrying an L-shaped pipe. The horizontal part of the duct is positioned beneath the float and

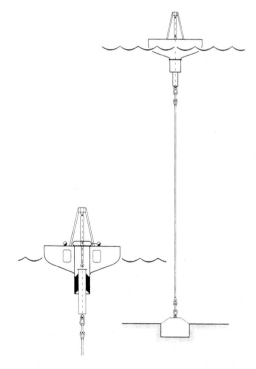

**Figure 11.2** Danish Point Absorber. (Courtesy of Caddet.)

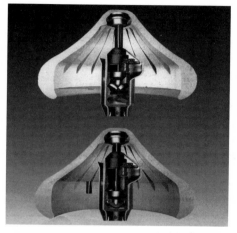

**Figure 11.3** Archimedes hoods in the raised and lowered positions. (Courtesy of Caddet.)

open at the rear. The vertical section is closed at the top and connected to an air turbine which operates when the device is moved by wave action. The final version is expected to be 20 m long (see Fig. 11.5).

Finally there is the WavePlane. This is a triangular-shaped floating device that is anchored at its central position. A series of grilles along the device facing the waves admit water to a horizontal pipe in a spiral flow. The torque thus created is converted into mechanical energy by a special turbine. This energy can either generate electricity or oxygenate the lower depths of polluted lakes or fjords. So far a 1:5-scale modified version has been operating in a fjord in Jutland (see Fig. 11.6).

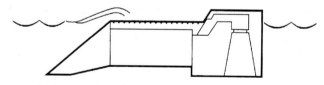

**Figure 11.4** Wave Dragon concept. (Courtesy of Caddet.)

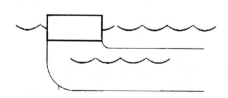

**Figure 11.5** The Swan DK3 'Backward Bend Duct Buoy'. (Courtesy of Caddet.)

**Figure 11.6**   The WavePlane. (Courtesy of Caddet.)

Unfortunately the latest information is that a recently elected government in Denmark has stopped further work on this programme. As an endorsement of its reversal of policy it has appointed a leading global-warming sceptic to a key environmental post.

## Oscillating water column

At Port Kembla in Australia a wave energy device which is a variation on the oscillating water column (OWC) principle is now operational. It was designed to be installed against the sea side of harbour walls or rocky peninsulas where there is deep water. A parabola-shaped wave concentrator extends into the sea, amplifying the waves by a factor of three by the time they reach the focal point. There they enter an air-filled chamber, forcing the air forwards and drawing it backwards through an aperture leading to a turbine as the waves arrive and then retreat. The angle of the turbine blades is adjusted via a sensor system so that they rotate in the same direction regardless of the direction of the air flow. This involves a pressure transducer which measures the pressure exerted on the ocean floor by each wave as it enters the chamber. A voltage signal proportional to the pressure is sent to a programmable logic controller (PLC) indicating the height and duration of each wave. The PLC adjusts the blade angle through a series of pinions and planet gears. A motion software program ensures that the information from the pressure transducer is translated into the optimal blade position at any given moment (see Fig. 11.7).

The Port Kembla installation has a peak capacity 500 kW and an output of over 1 GWh/year that is fed to the grid. The economics of the system compare favourably with solar energy and wind power. With refinements to the system the unit price is expected to outclass all competitors.

A single installation of this kind has the potential to generate 1000 kW which would power 2000 homes (Caddet). Several sites in Australia such as the Bass Strait and Southern Australia coast have the wave potential to generate up to 1 MW per unit.

In the right location, wave energy is more consistent and thus less intermittent energy source than either wind or solar. It causes no pollution and by offsetting the fossil generation saved by the plant, the savings in carbon dioxide are around 790 tonnes/year.

**Figure 11.7** Computer generated image of Port Kembla installation. (Courtesy of Caddet.)

## Large-scale tidal energy

This sector of the spectrum of renewables was considered in some detail in *Architecture in a Climate of Change*.[2] Since that book was written there has been something of a climate of change in official attitude to tidal energy, though there is still a barrier to overcome with regard to estuary systems. At the risk of reprehensible repetition, the case has to be put repeatedly in favour of a technology which overcomes most of the problems associated with barrage schemes. It is known as the 'tidal fence' which can be conceived as a bridge with numerous supports. Vertical or horizontal axis turbines are contained within a concrete structure which allows the free flow of water at all times. The 'fence' does reduce the cross-sectional area of an estuary location thereby increasing the rate of flow by up to a factor of four. It is a system as efficient in tidal streams and coastal currents as on an estuary site. Many offshore situations have the potential to generate 10 MW/km², and the UK is one of the most favoured of all locations in this respect. Of all the renewable technologies, large-scale tidal is one of the most likely candidates as a substitute for a new generation of nuclear plants. Spread around the most suitable locations with varying tide times this system could provide reliable base load electricity for an electricity infrastructure which will become increasingly reliant on intermittent suppliers (see Fig. 11.8).

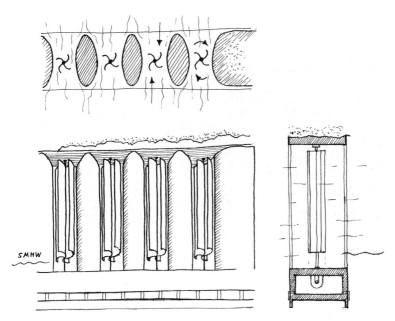

**Figure 11.8**  Tidal fence estuary turbines.

## Notes

1.  Smith PF. *Architecture in a Climate of Change*, pp. 28–32. Oxford: Architectural Press, 2001.
2.  Smith PF. *op cit.*, pp. 22–27.

# 12 Prospects for the energy infrastructure

The system of generating and distributing electricity is undergoing a slow, but radical change. In political science there is a concept called the 'elitist perspective' which describes how individuals and groups assume control over social institutions. Elitist clusters exert power through the manipulation of individuals and governments to achieve their aims and maximize their profits. This is graphically illustrated by the $20 million given by US energy companies between 1999 and 2002 to politicians. Their reward was that 36 representatives from the energy industry were consulted by the Bush administration over future energy policy but no consumer or environmental groups were represented.[1] World-wide energy companies share with pharmaceutical companies the pole position of influence over governments and continents. They will take concerted action when faced with a threat, as, for instance, by the phenomenon of global warming. Everything possible was done to undermine the credibility of the thousands of scientists who contributed to the three United Nations IPCC Scientific Reports on climate change.

Now, in the electricity supply and distribution sector their monopoly is being threatened by three major changes, which emerged during the end of the twentieth century. They have been defined by Carl J Weinberg as:

- *Governance*. There has been a growing trend to admit competition and market-based approaches to the supply of energy. A consequence of this has been an erosion of central control in favour of diversified market-based enterprises. This has introduced consumers to the concept of choice in the buying of energy.
- *The environment*. There is growing support for the principle of sustainable development and an awareness of the environmental consequences

of the unconstrained use of fossil fuels. The latter twentieth century saw an emphasis on the limitations of the carrying capacity of the earth and the fact that, for the first time in history, a single species has changed the geophysical balance of the planet. The electricity supply industry will increasingly come under pressure as the major emitter of carbon dioxide, the most abundant of human-induced greenhouse gases. Nature, it seems, has offered us a Faustian deal in the form of almost unlimited fossil-based energy for the next 100 years or more while ensuring that, if we take the deal, we will devastate the planet.
- *Technology.* There has been rapid progress in the development of renewable technologies and the emergence of smaller, modular, flexible technologies tailored to the needs of individual consumers and managed by information technology that threaten the hegemony of the big power utilities.

Again Weinberg:

> *The conceptual model of a utility as large central power plants connected to [its] customers by wires may well not be the model for the future. This is particularly true for developing countries.*[2]

It is inherently difficult for large organizations with their bureaucratic hierarchies, their investment in plant and a large workforce tied-in to a particular technology to adapt to radical change demanded by so-called 'disruptive technologies' like renewables. Furthermore, what is the incentive if they are still making substantial profits? Studies of technical innovation have revealed that radical innovations have never been introduced by market leaders.[3]

The state of California offers an example of how the market can rebel against the power of the utilities in response to increased gas prices, spiralling electricity costs – up to 40–50 cents/kWh – and insecurity of supply. Renewables suppliers offered a price of 8.5 cents/kWh fixed for 3 years. In other states wind energy electricity producers have offered 10–15-year contracts at 3–4 cents/kWh. Such low prices coupled with protection from the volatility of the utilities market are proving a most effective stimulus in attracting people to the renewables option.

In parallel with the awakening of this new concept of energy supply in the US there has been a marked shift away from large, centralized generating plants to smaller, more localized units. In the 1970s the average output of power stations reached 150 MW resulting from new large-scale nuclear and coal technology. With the decline of nuclear and the advent of independent power producers the average fell to 29 MW in the first half of the 1990s. So, already the energy infrastructure is moving in the direction of distributed and differentiated supply which should flag a warning to governments that are planning large nuclear power plants for the future. They will be pushing against the tide.

Increasingly power plants are being manufactured in assembly lines rather than constructed on site. They are available for small- and medium-sized businesses and domestic users. The ultimate shift will come when fuel cells become economic and hydrogen readily available. The market is being stimulated, not just by green imperatives, but also by concerns about reliability and quality. The steady movement away from a 'resources' economy to a 'knowledge' economy is at the heart of this demand for quality and reliability. This embraces both the information dependent enterprises like the financial markets and production-centred industries which rely on micro-processors. The Americans call this the 7/9ths problem, i.e. 99% plus five nines. The grid can only provide 4/9ths reliability which translated means 99.99% reliability. This may seem adequate, but can result in significant losses due to down time. For example, for credit card operators it can amount to $2,580,000 per hour and for stock brokers $6,480,000 per hour. In these circumstances minutes count yet the total adds up to about 8 hours per year. What these operations require is 7/9th or 99.99999% reliability. When electricity storage facilities like advanced batteries and flywheels match small-scale production technologies, we can expect the distributed alternative to invade the electricity production market.

This, of course, will be emphatically opposed by the large utilities who will see their revenue streams threatened. One of their weapons is in setting interconnection requirements which fall under two headings: technical standards and administration. The technical standards relate to ensuring compatibility and quality before a supplier can be linked to the grid. At present the tendency is for the burden of proof that a proposed connection to the grid will not harm the system rests with the supplier not the utility. It is raising the issue that there must be national standards if distributed generation is to have an impact on the future. The same goes for administrative issues concerning how a system is to be inspected and certified, and, above all, the rate at which an independent generator is paid.

In the USA 32 states have instituted 'net metering' which involves a small independent supplier having a meter capable of going into reverse so that the utility buys back power at the same price it sells to consumers. This is a facility urgently needed in the UK to stimulate the renewables market.

The ultimate configuration of energy supply may be the formation of numerous mini-grids enabling a much more precise matching of supply with demand within a local area. There may be various interconnections between mini-grids and with the national grid. Drawing from the national grid would be regulated by specified conditions such as using the grid only for baseload requirements. Information technology is now capable of managing the complexities of a system with a large number of distributed resources without centralized control. It can deal with the interplay of supply and demand providing hour by hour least cost outcomes to the benefit of consumers.

In the UK this fundamental reconfiguring of the energy supply system has been endorsed by the Royal Commission on Environmental Pollution which recommends:

> *a shift from very large all electricity plant towards more numerous combined heat and power plants. The electricity system will have to undergo major changes to cope with this development and with the expansion of smaller scale, intermittent renewable energy sources. The transition towards a low-emission energy system would be greatly helped by the development of new means of storing energy on a large scale.*[4]

The Washington Worldwatch Institute has also endorsed this scenario stating that 'an electricity grid with many small generators is inherently more stable than a grid serviced by only a few large plants'. That was before 11 September 2001 and the terrorist attack on the World Trade Center. Now the security of such plants has become a major issue. A dispersed system with many thousands of suppliers is immune to catastrophic failure.

It is unfortunate that many governments still consider renewables to be a side show in the scenarios for the energy future. Fossil fuels and nuclear are still perceived as the dominant players for next half century which means a commitment to a centralized grid system operated by a small number of large utilities. Numerous factors are now making small-scale renewable generation attractive and this trend will escalate as the technologies improve and pressures to reduce carbon dioxide emissions increases as evidence of climate change mounts. It would be the height of folly to commit to a system for decades to come which is highly vulnerable and which is already being supplanted by a wide range of renewable technologies which, for countries like the UK, could meet all energy needs, provided there is an energetic campaign to reduce demand. Because ultimately 'an electron saved is the cleanest option'.[5]

## Towards a hydrogen economy

Over the millennia there have been three ages of energy. First there was the epoch of wood burning lasting up to the eighteenth century when it was gradually supplanted by coal. The early twentieth century saw a gradual shift from coal to oil. The fourth energy age is dawning and will focus on hydrogen. Its drivers will be concern about security of supply of fossil fuels, anxieties about the environment especially global warming and, finally, advances in technology.

The concept of a hydrogen economy emerged from a group of General Motors engineers in the 1970s. However, at that time there was little incentive to switch from hydrocarbon fuels. Now things are different for a range of reasons.

The year 2001 marked the point at which the Gulf states controlled over 35% of world oil production. The significance of this figure is that it is said to be at a level at which a cartel of producers can control world oil prices. In the 1970s the world experienced two oil shocks engineered by the oil producers. The UK government has been warned that another similar oil shock could trigger a stock market collapse or even war. Since the 11 September outrage that possibility has loomed larger.

All this makes hydrogen the most attractive option as the energy carrier for the future. Used for powering a fuel cell its only by-products are heat and water. Even the executive director of GM Cars has conceded that 'our long term vision is of a hydrogen economy'. To reinforce this his company together with Ford, Daimler-Chrysler, Honda and Toyota are racing to be the first to market a fuel cell car by 2004. The President of Texaco Technology Ventures informed a US Scientific Committee of the House of Representatives that:

> *Market forces, greenery and innovation are shaping the future of our industry and propelling us inexorably towards hydrogen energy.*

The viability of a hydrogen economy is also linked inexorably to the fortunes of the fuel cell. This is why enormous research resources are directed towards reducing the unit cost and raising the efficiency of all types of fuel cell.

There are two approaches to the adoption of hydrogen as the prime energy carrier of the future. The first is to extract hydrogen from a readily available fuel like natural gas or petrol. As stated earlier, this is done by a reformer unit. The sage of the green movement, Amory Lovins, claims that a reformer the size of a water heater 'can produce enough hydrogen to serve the fuel cells in dozens of cars'. The great advantage of this approach is that there already exists the infrastructure for natural gas which has the highest hydrogen content of all the candidates for reforming hydrogen. This could equally apply to buildings, with an individual house accommodating a reformer/fuel cell package which would supply both heat and power. In future, garages could reform natural gas on site to make it available at the pump. The downside is that readily accessible gas reserves are diminishing and the UK faces the prospect of buying 90% of its gas from nations on whom it would prefer not to be reliant.

Another problem is that, if there is a substantial investment in a national system involving the reforming of natural gas, there is the danger that this will 'lock-out' the direct use of hydrogen produced by electrolysis. From a renewable energy and environmental point of view the technological 'lock-in' of an inferior technology would be most regrettable.

An infrastructure carrying hydrogen produced directly from electrolysis is the second option. This poses the 'chicken and egg' problem. Manufacturers will not invest heavily in the development of fuel cells until there is the network of pipes to serve a critical mass of consumers. On the other hand infrastructure providers will be loath to develop a network until fuel cells are cost effective and have a strong foothold in the market.

Some experts claim that the incremental path to the hydrogen economy is the only realistic approach, arguing that a complete hydrogen infrastructure built from scratch would be prohibitively expensive. This argument is attractive to governments who would be expected to bear some of the capital costs of the enterprise. Others disagree claiming that converting a natural gas network would not be 'prohibitively expensive' and that there would be economic and environmental costs associated with adopting a compromise solution with its lock-in risks.

As a distributed energy system matures, and PV and fuel cell efficiencies improve, so also will the opportunity for operators of domestic size renewable installations to direct their electricity to a neighbourhood electrolyser unit with reformer backup to produce hydrogen to feed a community fuel cell which would, in turn, provide the cluster of homes with heat and power.

Such dedicated PV/hydrogen installations already exist. One example is in operation in Neunburg vorm Wald, Germany.

Solar energy offers one of the most abundant sources of electrolysed hydrogen. Deserts flanking the Mediterranean have already been mentioned as the ideal location for parabolic trough or parabolic dish reflectors to produce high pressure steam to power steam turbines or Stirling engines to create the power to split water. The export of PV and solar hydrogen could transform the economies of some developing countries.

## Hydrogen storage

This is the final hurdle for the hydrogen economy to negotiate before it reaches the final straight. Fuel cells depend on a steady supply of hydrogen which means that storage backup is an essential component of the system where reformation is not involved.

The conventional storage method for hydrogen is pressurized tanks. The pressure varies according to volume: up to 50 litres requires 200–250 bar; larger amounts, 500–600 bar. Some very large containers can be as low as 16 bar.

It can be stored as a liquid but this necessitates cooling to −253°C and requires a heavily insulated tank.

Bonded hydrogen is another option. Granular metal hydrides store hydrogen by bonding it chemically to the surface of the material. The metal particles are charged by being heated and then receiving the hydrogen at high pressure. Some metals can absorb up to one thousand times their volume of hydrogen. On cooling the hydrogen is locked into the metal and released by heating. The heat may come from a high temperature fuel cell. For storage in buildings the most appropriate metal hydride is probably iron-titanium. It is too heavy for vehicle application but ideal for buildings having a relatively low operating temperature.

Recently interest has been aroused by a storage technology which has emerged from Japan and Hong Kong. It consists of nanotubes of carbon, that is, sheets of carbon rolled into minute tubes 0.4 nm (0.4 billionths of a metre) in diameter. This is just the size to accommodate hydrogen atoms. A pack of carbon nanotubes has the potential to store up to 70% of hydrogen by weight compared to 2–4% of metal hydrides. Research is progressing into nanofibre graphite which could be a winner provided the team at Northeastern University in Boston can surmount its predilection for water over hydrogen.

A more exotic possibility was reported in *Scientific American* in May 2000. It referred to the capacity of solid molecular hydrogen to turn to metal at a pressure of 400–620 GPa (4–6 million atmospheres). Solid metallic hydrogen can store huge amounts of energy which is released as it returns to the gas phase.

If, as seems likely, the global warming curve is steeper than the official projections, then the pressure to switch to a hydrogen economy will become irresistible. Fortune will favour those countries who have developed a strong manufacturing base for a range of renewables which will be in heavy demand, not least in the developing countries. The problem of the two billion of the world's population who do not have access to electricity can only be solved by renewables and a distributed supply system.

The country which is on course to become the first hydrogen economy because it has a head start with its immense resources of geothermal and hydro-power is Iceland. It plans to convert all cars, trucks, buses and boats to hydrogen over the next 30 years. It will also export hydrogen to Europe. Even more ambitious is the island of Vanuata in the Pacific Ocean. It is en route to achieve a 100% hydrogen economy by 2010 due to its abundance of renewable resources: geothermal, wind, solar and hydro-power. Not to be outdone, Hawaii which is rich in solar and geothermal resources (and, no doubt, wave) recently established a public–private partnership to promote hydrogen as a major player in the island's economy, even exporting the gas to California.

## Regenerative fuel cell

Regenesys is a technology which is about to receive its first large-scale demonstration. It converts electrical energy to chemical energy and is capable of storing massive amounts of electricity. Energy is stored in concentrated aqueous electrolyte solution, sodium bromide and dodium polysulphide. On charging, the bromide ions are oxidized to bromine while sulphur in the polysulphide anions is converted to sulphide ions. On discharging, the sulphide ions act as the reducing agent and the tribromide ion as the oxidizing agent. The system can be switched from fully charging to discharging in about 20 ms.

A 360 GJ Regenesys energy storage system is under construction in the UK. It will have a rated power output of 15 MW which will feed directly into ths grid.

In the opinion of the Royal Commission of Environmental Pollution, hydrogen and regenerative fuel cells will be in widespread operation by the middle of the century. If global warming and security supply issues simultaneously become critical then viable large-scale storage technologies will arrive much sooner.

## Combined heat and power (CHP)

From time to time reference has been made in the text to CHP. Since there seems to be strong European Union and UK government support for this system of energy distribution it calls for special consideration.

First, electricity generation in the UK is the largest single contributor to carbon dioxide emissions, amounting to 26% of the total. Many buildings are responsible for more carbon dioxide from the electricity they use than from the fuel for the boilers providing hot water and space heating. At the same time the heat from power stations is rejected to cooling towers and thence to rivers and the sea. The River Trent in the UK is almost suitable for tropical fish.

CHP can be scaled to meet almost any level of demand from a single home to a whole city. Already some cities like Sheffield receive heat and power from the incineration of municipal waste. However, this is not an ideal heat and power source for the future on account of its emissions. Importantly the infrastructure exists to be converted in the future to more environmentally benign producers of heat and power.

The European Commission aims to double the use of CHP by 2010. The UK government has a target of 10 GWe of CHP with associated carbon savings of 6 million tonnes per year which represents 25% of its declared target savings or 20% by 2010.

A basic division in providing CHP is between factory-produced units up to 1 MWe and custom-built site-specific plants producing up to hundreds of megawatts. Rapid developments in the technology of small gas turbines and gas engines is helping to create favourable conditions for CHP which have an efficiency exceeding 70%. According to David Green, Director of the CHP Association, a typical payback time for CHP is 3–5 years with an operating life of 15–20 years.

As stated earlier the UK is on the verge of seeing a single-home CHP package based on a Stirling engine reaching market status. Community CHP systems using turbines powered by natural gas or, preferably, biogas from anaerobic digestion plants are a viable system now and could take off with the right government support. Housing estates now being built throughout the UK should be provided at the outset with an insulated hot-water pipe infrastructure even though the system may not be operational initially. It is much more cost effective to use a common trench at the construction stage than retrofit when the external works are complete.

The ultimate opportunity is for city-wide CHP. A genuine commitment to a sustainable future would require a government to promote and subsidize city-wide CHP using large, low temperature water grids as used successfully in Denmark.

One option being proposed is to exploit the waste heat from large coal- and oil-fired or nuclear power stations. Nuclear power is enormously wasteful of heat, producing much more excess heat per unit of power than conventional power stations. Plants of this size are usually some distance from conurbations. However, Denmark again provides the prototype with the city of Århus receiving heat from a coal-fired plant 30 km distant. The rate of flow is around 3 m/s through large diameter pipes.

However, with pressure increasing for the electricity infrastructure to evolve into a much more fragmented, distributed system, this would not be a wise investment. The capital commitment would inhibit conversion to a fundamentally different distribution system. This would be especially alarming in the case of nuclear power since it would establish a cost effective argument (however flawed) for replacing the aging nuclear plants with a new generation of nuclear power stations. The route ahead is for near zero carbon CHP plants fuelled by wood from rapid rotation crops or biogas from farm and municipal waste and the anaerobic conversion of sewage The ultimate CHP technology at city scale must be high temperature fuel cells fed with direct piped hydrogen, but that is decades in the future.

CHP has advantages when used in conjunction with solar energy and wind power. Large plants between 100 and 300 MW of electrical capacity are flexible, having the ability to change their mode of operation from producing electricity alone to delivering both electricity and heat in varying proportions. This means that it can adjust its mode according to how much electricity is being provided from renewable sources. CHP is reliably available at times of system peak being immune to the vagaries of wind or sun. It is therefore ideal for complementing renewable technologies.

There is a final twist to CHP. It can also provide cooling in so-called 'trigeneration' mode. Most trigeneration schemes are to be found in cities in the US where air-conditioning accounts for considerable electricity consumption. Piped chilled water can significantly reduce the electricity demand from air-conditioning plants in large office complexes. Even a number of financial institutions in the City of London enjoy this facility.

## Barriers to progress

A drawback which affects most renewables is the New Electricity Trading Arrangement (NETA). This requires a provider of electricity to the grid to estimate in advance how much electricity they will be exporting.

Suppliers who may be subject to quite large fluctuations in output due to the inconsistency of wind or sun are severely disadvantaged by this regulation.

Secondly, the UK conforms with the European Union in the way heat and power from CHP are evaluated. It is the heat which has prime value; the electricity is treated as a waste product which is a mechanism which Alice would recognize from Wonderland. It is like saying that the heat from a car radiator is of prime value and the distance travelled a worthless by-product.

Finally, another disparity is the payback time imposed on CHP which is 6 years. The new Part L of the Building Regulations (England and Wales) brought into force in April 2002 require insulation standards in buildings which produce a payback time of 16 years. This is analogous to the discount rate imposed on renewable technologies which severely prejudice high capital cost but long-life low running cost renewables like tidal energy. These are devices conceived by economists which take no account of benefits like reducing carbon dioxide emissions, low level pollution that affects health, or long-term revenue gains.

It is essential that there is now consistency between the words of politicians in backing CHP and their actions in facilitating its widespread adoption. For a start, electricity from CHP must be ascribed its full value and that the contribution of embedded generation generally is fully acknowledged in legislation and in the returns which it offers to suppliers.

## Conclusion

While the UK expresses its commitment to the principle of distributed generation with contributions from thousands, perhaps millions of contributors, in reality the dice is heavily loaded against small-scale generation and CHP. For example:

- There is a complex and lengthy process to be undertaken before a small contributor can be accepted by a distribution network operator (DNO).
- All the costs of providing the hardware for connection are borne by the small contributor.
- The UK government will not acknowledge what the real market situation is *vis-à-vis* renewables as against fossil fuels. First, renewables must be compensated for the avoided costs of pollution. Second, fossil fuels must have their subsidies removed. According to the Organization for Economic Co-operation and Development (OECD) 2002 report we are subsidizing fossil-based energy to the tune of $57 billion per year. The report states: "Through the provision of subsidies on fossil fuels, governments are effectively subsidizing pollution and global warming as more than 60% of all subsidies flow to oil, coal and gas". The playing field is going to take a lot of levelling.

True, it is offering a subsidy for the development of PV – up to 1000 roofs. By comparison, Germany has a programme to equip 100,000 roofs by 2003. To achieve this there are low interest loans (1.9% in 2001) and a bonus on the buy-back price. In 1999 the federal government introduced the Law for the Priority of Renewable Energy (REL). It came into operation in April 2000 with a buy-back price of €0.51/kWh. The aim is to achieve installed power of 300 MWp by 2003. The effect has been dramatic. For example, in Bavaria the installed PV capacity in 1999 was 2350 kW. In 2001 it had become 21,730 kW. The only limiting factor seems to be the capacity of the 30 PV manufacturers in Germany to meet the demand.

The stark truth is that small scale renewables and distributed generation will never take off in the UK while it has to compete with the depressed prices of fossil fuels. There are gestures in the right direction with DNOs being required to take a percentage of their energy from major renewables sources like wind or biomass. However, the only way that the situation could be rectified in favour of small-scale renewables is for the example of Germany to be followed or for there to be a Europe-wide carbon tax which recognizes the external costs associated with fossil fuels. Neither seem likely. To paraphrase St Augustine: 'Lord grant us distributed generation – but not just yet'.

## Notes

1. *The Guardian*, 27 March 2002.
2. Keeping the lights on; sustainable scenarios for the future, *Renewable Energy World*, July–August 2001, pp. 36–37.
3. Christensen CM. *The Innovators Dilemma. When New Technologies Cause Great Firms to Fall*. Cambridge, MA: Harvard Business School Press, 1997.
4. 22nd report *Energy, The Changing Climate*, p. 169. London: Stationery Office, 2000.
5. Dunn S. *Renewable Energy World*, July–August 2001.

# 13 Materials

## Concrete

As possibly the most extensively used building material, concrete attracts criticism from environmentalists on account of its carbon intensive production techniques and its use of a once-only natural resource, limestone. Cement is formed by heating clay and lime in a rotary kiln to a temperature of about 1450°C which produces some 3000 kg/tonne of carbon dioxide. In addition, the heating process produces a chemical reaction through the conversion of calcium carbonate into calcium oxide that releases about 2200 kg of carbon dioxide. Add to this the carbon miles in transportation, the impacts caused by mining, etc. and concrete gains few points on the sustainability scale.

The UK Climate Change Levy is providing a powerful incentive for manufacturers to reduce carbon dioxide emissions since an 80% abatement of the tax can be granted in return for specific carbon dioxide abatement strategies. One method of reducing concrete's carbon impact is to use pulverized fuel ash (PVA) to reduce the proportion of cement in the concrete mix. These new blended cements contain up to 30% of PVA a by-product of coal-fired electricity generation. This use of PVA has the further advantage of avoiding landfill costs while also reducing the need to quarry natural aggregates such as gravel. However, it must be remembered that it is the waste product of carbon-intensive coal-fired power stations. It also contains some toxic chemicals. Its availability will decline as coal-fired power stations are phased out.

The mountains of slate waste which encircle Blaenau Ffestioniog in north Wales are destined to become a powdered aggregate in the near future. This will offer the double benefit of avoiding depleting a natural resource and also drastically improving the amenity value of an area scarred by slate mining over the centuries.

The development of the technology of geopolymers offers the prospect of a more eco-friendly concrete. Geopolymerization is a geosynthesis which is a reaction that chemically bonds minerals to form molecules that are structurally comparable to the molecules which provide the strength to rocks. In the opinion of Jean Davidovits of the French Geopolymer Institute at St Quentin these 'geopolymeric' concretes would reduce carbon dioxide emissions associated with conventional concrete by 80–90%. This is said to be due to the avoidance of calcination from calcium carbonate and the lower kiln temperature of 750°C. The market availability of this material is said to be at least 5 years away (see www.geopolymer.org).

Recycled crushed concrete has been used for some time for low-grade applications like road construction. It is now being heralded as being suitable for less-demanding structural elements. One attraction of this material is that it gains a BREEAM (Building Research Establishment Environmental Assessment Method) credit if used in sufficient quantity. The main disadvantage of the material concerns quality control. A consignment may contain concrete from numerous sites which means that each batch must be tested by being sieved and chemically analysed to check its ingredients and quality (see www.bre.co.uk).[1]

## Glass

The RIBA conference that initiated this book included the introduction by Pilkington Architectural of their Triple Planar glass. This is a glazing system that eliminates the need for framing with the junction between panes sealed with 10–12 mm of silicon. The importance of this system is that it can achieve a U-value of 0.8 W/m$^2$ K that should make it highly attractive for commercial application when coupled with its aesthetic appeal (see www.pilkington.com/planar).

A wider market can be expected for Pilkington's electrochromic glass marketed as Econtrol. This works by passing a low electrical voltage across a microscopically thin coating to the glass activating a tungsten-bearing electrochromic layer which can darken in stages. Electricity is only used to change the state of the coating, not to sustain its level of transmittance. About 3 V are needed to effect the change, and this could be provided by the building energy management system or be individually controlled by occupants, allowing for fine-tuning to immediate needs. PV cells integrated into a façade or roof could easily supply this level of power.

This system offers several advantages. Foremost is the fact that it can save energy. It avoids overheating and solar glare. Trials conducted in Germany indicated that it can save up to 50% of the energy required for air-conditioning. Even when the glass is fully darkened external views are not impaired. The avoided cost of external shading must also be factored into the cost-benefit analysis.

The first building to feature Econtrol was a bank in Dresden. The electrochromic glazing on the southern elevation is over 17 m high and 8 m wide. The glass can be switched to give five levels of light and heat transmittance.

Finally, in 2002, Pilkington introduced 'hydrophilic' glass to the market. This is a self-cleaning glass which goes under the name of Pilkington Activ. Layers are deposited on the glass during the float manufacturing process to produce the photocatalytic characteristics of the glass. After exposure to ultraviolet light in daylight the coating reacts chemically in two ways. First it breaks down organic deposits – tree sap, bird droppings, etc. – by introducing extra molecules of oxygen into the deposit. This has the effect of accelerating the rate of decay. Second, the coating causes the glass to become hydrophilic. This means that droplets of rain coalesce to form sheets of water which slide down the glass removing dirt particles in the process. The really smart aspect of the product is that the coating stores enough ultraviolet energy during the day to sustain the process overnight.

The avoidance of cleaning costs, especially for commercial buildings, could offer considerable annual savings, especially where atria are concerned. For householders it could, in the long term, spell the end of the local, friendly window cleaner.

Now that nanotechnology has taken a hold on glass manufacturers all kinds of possibility can be envisaged like glass that responds instantly to changes in weather or that is an integrated photovoltaic electricity generator.

## Insulation

There is an increasing demand for eco-insulation materials that are obtained from natural sources. The most popular up to the present is cellulose fibre derived from recycled newspaper. The material is treated with boron to give fire resistance and protect against vermin infestation. It is suitable for wet-spray or dry blown application. One of the most popular proprietory brands is 'Warmcell', supplied by Excel Industries which belongs to Fillcrete. It has a thermal conductivity of 0.036 W/m K which puts it in the same category as most of the main insulants on the market. It has BBA (British Board of Agrèment) certification. Warmcell is an integral part of Fillcrete's 'breathing wall' panel system suitable for structural walls, floor and roof components. The panels have a U-value of 0.19 W/m² K. The panels incorporate service ducts on the internal face to facilitate rapid on-site fixture of services.

Prefabrication is becoming increasingly popular. This is because elements are produced in controlled conditions and safe from the elements. Because of their extremely tight tolerances they can offer guaranteed air tightness which is a prerequisite for highly energy efficient buildings.

Other manufacturers of cellulose fibre insulation include Construction Resources supplying Isofloc and 'Save It' (Nottingham) producing Ecofibre. These also are BBA certified.

Coming more into prominence is sheep's wool. One of the first buildings to use wool as an insulant was the exhibition House of the Future within the Museum of Welsh Life in south Wales. It uses 200 mm of wool in its cavities. At the time it had to be imported from France. Now the UK has its own treatment facilities and can be obtained from the Wool Marketing Board. It has to be treated with water-based boron.

The most ambitious use of sheep's wool for insulation in the UK is in what is claimed to be the largest commercial eco-building in the UK being erected by the Centre for Alternative Technology (CAT) at Machynlleth, Wales. The installed thickness is 325 mm and the wool was hand sprayed with boron during installation.

A demonstration project in Scotland is currently being evaluated to test the effectiveness of hemp as an insulation material. The verdict so far is that the hemp homes are using significantly less energy than was predicted by the SAP ratings and U-value calculations. They are consistently outperforming the control houses which have conventional masonry construction with cavity insulation. This is a material to watch.

Natural Building Technologies of High Wycombe was established to promote the widespread use of natural building products. These include cellulose fibre, cork and sheep's wool. All these natural materials are hygroscopic, that is, they absorb moisture without any damage to their functional integrity. Water vapour can move through them that makes them ideal for 'breathing' walls which offer short-term protection against condensation. The big benefit is in offsetting the need for vapour barriers which are notorious for being at the mercy of operatives on site.

The emergence of transparent insulation materials (TIMs) offers the double benefit of providing insulation and space heating. One product, StoTherm Solar consists of a honeycomb structure of glass-coated polycarbonate. It is produced by the external insulation specialists Sto AG. It is claimed that a southerly façade using StoTherm Solar could achieve an energy gain of 120 kW h/m$^2$ per year. In winter the outside temperature might  be as low as −10°C. Despite this, the back of the TIM could be as high as 60°C, benefiting from the low angle of the sun. Since the TIM is bonded to the inner wall surface this warmth would be transmitted to the interior, producing a room temperature of around 20°C. That is on the assumption that the wall is of solid construction with a density of at least 1200 kg/m$^3$. Even on north-facing elevations this technology could offer an energy gain of up to 40 kW h/m$^2$ per year.

Saving energy is one thing; buildings as carbon sinks is another, yet this is the destiny of buildings according to John Harrison, a technologist from Hobart, Tasmania. He has produced a magnesium carbonate-based 'eco-cement'. In the first place it only uses half the energy for process heating required by calcium carbonate (Portland) cement. The roasting process produces carbon dioxide but most of this is reabsorbed by a process of carbonation as the cement hardens. Using eco-cement for such items as concrete blocks means that nearly all the material will eventually carbonate resulting in an absorption rate of 0.4 tonnes of carbon dioxide for every tonne of concrete. The ultimate eco-credential of this material is the rate of carbon sequestration. According to Harrison: 'The opportunities to use carbonation processes to sequester carbon from the air are just huge. It can take conventional cements centuries or even millennia to absorb as much as eco-cements can absorb in months'.[2] This means that an eco-concrete tower block can perform the same function as growing trees as it steadily fixes carbon. Harrison estimates that a shift to eco-cement could ultimately cut carbon dioxide emissions by over 1 billion tonnes since it could replace 80% of uses currently served by Portland cement.

There is one further attribute to this material. Being less alkaline than Portland cement it can incorporate up to four time more waste in the mix than conventional cement to provide bulk without losing strength. This could include organic waste which would otherwise be burnt or added to landfill, sawdust, plastics, rubber and fly ash.

Eco-cement is not unique in its pollution absorbing properties. Mitsubishi is producing paving slabs coated with titanium dioxide which remove most pollutants from the air. In Japan 50 towns are already using them and in Hong Kong it is estimated that they remove up to 90% of the nitrogen oxides that create smog. Magnesium-based concrete coated with titanium dioxide could be the basis for eco-cities of the future.

## Smart materials

Already a smart material has figured here, namely electrochromic glass.

According to Philip Ball, associate editor for physical sciences with the journal *Nature*:

> *Smart materials represent the epitome of the new paradigm of materials science whereby structural materials are being superseded by functional ones. Smart materials carry out their tasks as a result of their intrinsic properties. In many situations they will replace mechanical operations. We will see smart devices in which the materials themselves do the job of levers, gears and even electronic circuitry. There is even the prospect of a house built of bricks that change their thermal insulating properties depending on the outside temperature so as to maximise energy efficiency.[3]*

Materials such as thermochromic glass (darkens in response to heat) come into the general category of *passive* smart materials. The really exciting advances are in *active* smart materials. An active system is controlled not only by external forces but also by some internal signal. In smart systems an active response usually involves a feedback loop that enables the system to 'tune' its response and thus adapt to a changing environment rather than be passively driven by external forces. An example is a vibrating-damping smart system. Mechanical movement triggers a feedback loop into providing movement that stabilizes the system. As the frequency or amplitude of the vibrations change so the feedback loop modifies the reaction to compensate.

One useful class of smart materials are 'shape memory alloys' (SMAS) alternatively called 'solid-state phase transformations'. These are materials which, after deformation, return completely to their former shape. They function by virtue of the fact that the crystal structures of SMAS change when heated. An application already being exploited is as thermostats where bimetal strips are replaced by alloys. They can be incorporated into mechanisms for operating ventilation louvres or ventilation/heating diffusers.

In general, smart systems can be divided into sensors and actuators. Sensors are detection devices to respond to changes in the environment and warn accordingly. Actuators make things happen; they are control devices that close or open an electrical circuit or close or open a pipe. In fact they can be tailored to serve both functions. For example, they may perform a dual role extracting heat from low grade sources like ground water or geothermal reservoirs and serve as mechanical pumps to deliver the warmed water to the heating system of a building. No moving parts; no possibility of mechanical breakdown and all at low cost; it seems 'such stuff as dreams are made of' and may well transform the prospects for such technologies as heat pumps.

In principle SMAS can be used for any application which requires heat to be converted into mechanical action.

## Smart fluids

By introducing a strong electrical field, certain fluids can change to a near solid state. They are called 'electrorheological fluids' (rheology is the study of the viscosity and flow capacity of fluids). They can be made intelligent by coupling them to sensor devices which detect sudden movement. They have the potential to replace a range of mechanical devices such as vehicle clutches, springs and damping devices to eliminate mechanical vibrations.

Another class of smart fluid is activated by being exposed to a magnetic field. Linked to sensors they would be ideal for buildings in earthquake zones. Buildings would be constructed off concrete rafts which in turn would be supported by an array of magnetorheological dampers. At the onset of vibrations these would instantly change from solid to fluid and soak up the movement of the earth. In Tokyo and Osaka several recent buildings already exploit vibration damping and variable stiffness devices to counteract seismic movement.

There is yet another dimension to the characteristics of smart materials – materials that learn, that get smarter as they get older. They have an inbuilt degree of intelligence and are capable of optimizing their performance in response to feedback information.

What we will see in the near future are smart structures equipped with an array of fibre optic 'nerves' that will indicate what a structure is 'feeling' at any given moment and give instant information of any impending catastrophic failure. If the end of the last century was characterized by the rise of high technology with ever more complex electronic wizardry packed into ever smaller spaces, the future, according to materials scientists, 'may hold an increasing simplicity, as materials replace machines.'[4] We will learn to be adaptive rather than assertive. This surely is what environmental responsibility is all about.

## Notes

1. For further information refer to *Ecotech 5*, in association with *Architecture Today*, 5 May 2002.
2. 'Green Foundations', *New Scientist*, p. 40, 13 July 2002.
3. Ball P. *Made to Measure*, p. 104. Princeton, NJ: Princeton University Press, 1997.
4. Ball P. *op cit.*, p. 142.

# 14   The photonic revolution

The end of the twentieth century witnessed a transformation in the power of light. It has already revolutionized communications and promises to do the same for illumination, in both cases resulting in substantial savings in energy.

The micro-electronic transformation of the communications infrastructure which occurred over the last two decades is based on the capacity of semiconductors such as silicon to control electric currents. That control depends on a feature called the 'band gap' and it is the characteristics of that gap which determines which electrons are blocked from travelling through the semiconductor.

## The light emitting diode (LED)

Scientists have produced materials which have a photonic band gap, namely a range of wavelengths of light which are unable to pass through the material. This is achieved by structuring the materials in precisely designed patterns at the nanoscopic scale. The result has been called 'semiconductors of light'.

Light emitted from traditional forms of illumination is effectively a by-product of heat. The incandescent light bulb operates at 2000°C so clearly much of the energy it uses is wasted.

There is an alternative which leans heavily on quantum theory which states that an atom's electrons emit energy whenever they jump from a high to a low energy level. Provided that the difference between the two levels is in the right range, the surplus energy is manifest as a flash of light – a photon. The wavelength and thus the colour of the light is determined by the size of the energy gap and this, in turn, depends on the atoms involved.

The principle behind the semiconductor LED is that quantum transitions can take place within a solid. In an appropriate material some electrons are free to move while others are bound to the atoms. It is the difference between the energy state of these two types of electron which is termed the 'band gap'. The application of a small electric current to a diode made from a semiconductor raises electrons to a higher energy state. As the electrons pass through the band gap they generate photons at a wavelength determined by the size of the gap. An appropriate semiconductor produces photons in the visible spectrum to create the LED.

Up to the present it has not been possible to make an LED that emits pure white light. To get close to this goal a combination of LEDs emitting red, green and blue light mixes these hues to produce a warm white light. The blue light has been a stumbling block but recently researchers in Japan made a chip using the semiconductor gallium nitride which emits blue light. This completed the triad of hues.

One of the criteria for judging the quality of artificial light is the degree to which it approximates to sunlight. This is measured by a colour rendering index (CRI) in which 100 represents absolute affinity. Incandescent bulbs have a score of 95 against the best LEDs which achieve 85. However, it is at the level of efficiency that LEDs leave the rest of the field behind. Incandescent bulbs produce 10–20 lumens per watt while LEDs emit 100 lumens per watt. Furthermore, they have a life expectancy of about 50,000 hours. Their durability is measured in years perhaps even decades.

However, there is a problem with the whitish light produced by mixing blue, red and green LEDs in that the human eye is not as sensitive to light at the blue and red ends of the visible spectrum as it is to the green. Consequently much of the power used to generate blue and red light is wasted. This problem has been addressed by Frederick Schubert of the Center for Photonics Research at the University of Boston. In January 2000 it was reported that he had produced an LED which took into account the sensitivities of the human eye. The result was an LED emitting white light at the highest possible efficiency.

Schubert's answer was a device called a 'photon recycling semiconductor' (PRS-LED) that uses electrical power to generate photons at a single wavelength. Some of the photons are recycled to produce light at a different wavelength. The two wavelengths are calculated to produce the effect of white light. Schubert's device uses blue and orange to achieve this effect. The blue light is produced by an LED made of gallium, nitrogen and indium. The second semiconductor layer consists of gallium indium and phosphorus. The band gap of this second layer material has been adjusted to produce orange light. The claimed efficiency of this device is 330 lumens per watt (see Fig. 14.1).

This LED is still in the laboratory and the research effort is focused on improving its CRI and improving its efficiency so that a PRS-LED measuring less than a square centimetre will emit as much light as a 60-W bulb while using only 3 W of power. This highlights another virtue of this technology, its compactness. The absence of a glass bulb and bulky connections makes this a truly versatile form of illumination capable of being integrated

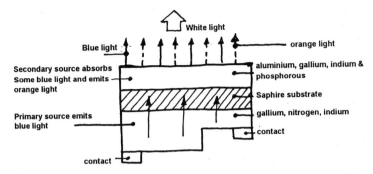

**Figure 14.1** The Schubert Photon Recycling Semiconductor (PRS-LED) (derived from *New Scientist* article 'The end of light as we know it', 8 January 2000).

into walls, ceilings and even floors. There are also moves to create LEDs which respond to changes in daylight level by adjusting their colour and brightness.

Even more radical is the suggestion by Ton Begemann of Eindhoven University that an LED lighting system might also be a carrier of information. He claims it would be possible to modulate the power supply to the LED in such a way as to enable it to carry digital information but at speeds too fast for the eye to detect. A pager, sensor or computer would be able to decode the message making the light on the desk a node in a communication system via the electricity supply network.

The greatest benefit of all would be in the saving of energy. In most commercial buildings lighting is the main consumer of electricity. Colin Humphreys, a materials scientist at Cambridge University, estimates that LEDs would cut lighting bills by 80%. The reduction in carbon dioxide emissions due to lighting would also approach that percentage. Transposed to the scale of a nation, if all the light sources in the US were converted to LEDs, this would cancel out the need for new power stations for 20 years, assuming the present rate of increase in electricity consumption of 2.7% per year.

As yet LEDs are not cost effective set against conventional light sources. A Schubert 60-W equivalent LED would cost $100. However, this is a technology which is bound to succeed, especially if the avoided cost of pollution and carbon dioxide emissions is factored into the cost-benefit analysis. Already 8% of US traffic signals use red LEDs. Developments in the technology coupled with economies of scale should enable LEDs to swamp the market within a decade. This will qualify them as one of the leading technologies in the fight to combat global warming.

## Photonics in communication

Fibre optics are now a familiar feature of long-range communication. An optical fibre consists of a glass core and a cladding layer wrapping around

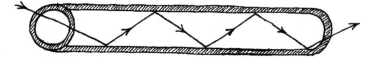

**Figure 14.2**   Optical fibre.

it. The core and cladding are precisely chosen so that their refractive indices (the ability to bend light by specific amounts) ensure that the photons within the core are always reflected at the interface of the cladding (see Fig. 14.2).

This ensures that the only way light can escape is through the ends of the fibre. Either an LED or a laser sends electronic data that have been converted to photons along the fibre at a wavelength of between 1200 and 1600 nm. The most advanced fibres can send a light signal for about 50 miles without the need to boost the signal. Until the early 1990s the boosters were electronic which created a bottleneck in the system. The answer was to insert stretches of fibre that were infused with ions of the rare earth erbium. When the erbium-doped fibres are irradiated by a laser light the excited ions refresh the fading signal. This has resulted in dramatic improvements in capacity and speed – up to tens of gigabits per second. At the same time this refreshing facility can boost the power of many wavelengths simultaneously, so that it is now possible to send 160 frequencies in parallel and supply a total bandwidth of 400 gigabits per second over a fibre. Visible on the horizon is a fibre capacity of 300–400 terabits a second. New technology could break the petabit barrier. It will not come a moment too soon.

In February 2000 the computer network at Kent State University in the US came to a virtual standstill when thousands of hits from the music file-sharing utility Napster invaded e-mails from the vice chancellor and research data on genetic engineering. This gives credence to the nightmare scenario that a video-Napster capable of downloading anything from *Birth of a Nation* to *Rocky IV* could bring down the entire Internet.[1] On-line virtual reality could overwhelm the system with up to 10 petabits per second which is 10,000 times greater than present day traffic (a petabit is ten to the power of 15 bits). Linked computers sharing power called metacomputing could require 200 petabit capacity.

The only transmission medium capable of meeting this challenge is a fibre optic system which is not inhibited by electronic switching. At present the problem is that the most advanced networks transmitting 10 billion bits per second threaten to choke the processing units and microchip memories in electronic switches. It is as though a ten-lane motorway suddenly contracts to a country lane. The gigabit tidal wave of photonic data has to be broken-up into slower data streams that can be converted to electronic processing. Then the sequence has to be reversed to produce the fast flowing photonic mode. The answer is photonic switching, the holy grail of photonics research.

Eliminating the electronic stage of transmission has been the aim of Japanese scientists in Tsukuba. In May 2001 they claimed to have created an optical transistor that would pave the way for all-optical networks. Basically they have found a way to make one light beam make another disappear, thereby creating an optical semiconductor.

Huge amounts of venture capital are being directed at this developing field of science. In the first 9 months of 2000 venture funding for optical networks totalled $3.4 billion. The attraction for this kind of investor is that the cost of transmitting a bit of optical information is halving every nine months.

Soon the whole world will be linked to an optical fibre superhighway based on photonic materials. One consequence is that teleworking will become much more prevalent, enabling commercial enterprises to scale down their centralized operations. High-capacity communication systems based on a multimedia supercorridor accommodating audio, computer and visual communication will have a major impact on work patterns. Already teleconferencing is reducing the need for costly gatherings of executives as companies spread their operations globally. This will offer much greater freedom to employees as regards their place of abode.

The most recent development in information technology is known as 'tele-immersion' described by *Scientific American* as 'a new telecommunications medium which combines virtual reality with video-conferencing. [It] aims to allow people separated by great distances to interact naturally as though they were in the same room' and 'involves monumental improvements in a host of computing technologies ... Within ten years tele-immersion could be a substitute for many types of business travel.[2]

Photonic switching is perhaps the most monumental improvement that heralds a quantum change in the architecture of computers which are already approaching the barrier imposed by the physics of electronic processing. Not only will this next generation of computers have vastly increased capacity, they will achieve this with a fraction of the power consumed by present-day machines. They will also avoid the heat gains of electronic processors. So the combination of LEDs and photonic computers will dramatically reduce the energy requirements of a typical office building, not only in terms of lighting and computing load but also in reducing the cooling load on the ventilation system.

A note of caution to conclude this chapter. One outcome of the exponential development of information technology is that the economic and business certainties of the twentieth century are disintegrating. As electronic commerce grows, governments will find it ever harder to raise taxes. Each day trillions of dollars move around the global money market as corporations locate their transactions in low tax jurisdictions. Add to this the fact that people are increasingly obtaining goods and services via the Internet from places with the lowest taxes and it is clear that national governments will have diminishing power to raise revenue, with obvious consequences for the social services.

One scenario is that the growing gap between the poor and the affluent will continue to widen. The dividing line will become sharply defined as between those with IT and communication skills who can keep up with the pace of change and those who increasingly fall behind in this new Darwinian environment. As Ian Angell (head of the Department of Information Systems, London School of Economics) puts it:

> *People with computer skills are likely to end up winners. Those without are likely to emerge as losers. The power of the nation state will weaken. Communities that invest substantially in communication technologies will thrive. Those who don't, or those whose citizens are isolated from the new ways to communicate, will suffer. Change is inevitable. The Information Age will be kindest to those who adapt.*[3]

## Notes

1. *Scientific American*, January 2001
2. *Scientific American*, p. 54, April 2001.
3. *New Scientist*, pp. 44–45, 4 March 2001.

# 15 Building integrated renewable energy: case studies

## Malmo: 'city of the future'

The development on the waterfront of this southern city in Sweden was given its initial impetus by an exhibition aimed at promoting sustainable urban development. The significance of this project is that it seeks to reconcile the goals of sustainable design with the demands of the market. Malmo is set to experience a renaissance in its fortunes with the completion of the Oresund Bridge linking Sweden to Denmark. This project represents an emphatic statement of intent as the new gateway to the rest of Europe.

The development occupies the Vastra Hamnen site formerly dedicated to industrial and dockside use. About 30 hectares is now occupied by a wide range of apartments by a selection of international architects including Ralph Erskine. The city laid down a number of conditions for the leases. The programme included statements about the overall character of the development including criteria for colours and ecological credibility of materials. An essential part of the development was the 'green space factor' providing parkland and foliage to compensate for the built-over area (see Fig. 15.1).

Building performance included the stipulation that energy use must be less than 105 kW h/m$^2$/year. The overall plan aims to obtain 100% of the community's electricity from renewable sources such as a 2 MW wind turbine and 120 m$^2$ of PVs (see Fig. 15.2).

A heat pump drawing warmth from an underground aquifer and sea water is anticipated to meet 83% of district heating needs. The same system will provide cooling in summer. Of the remaining heat demand around 15% will be provided by 2000 m$^2$ of solar collectors and the rest from biogas derived from waste and sewerage. The energy is distributed by district heating/cooling mains.

Another prerequisite was that there should be a mix of social and luxury accommodation. The market-led pressures ensured that the expensive properties had the best outlooks with views over the sea or canal. This means that most of the apartments have east–west facing glazing – a case of outlook taking precedence over solar orientation.

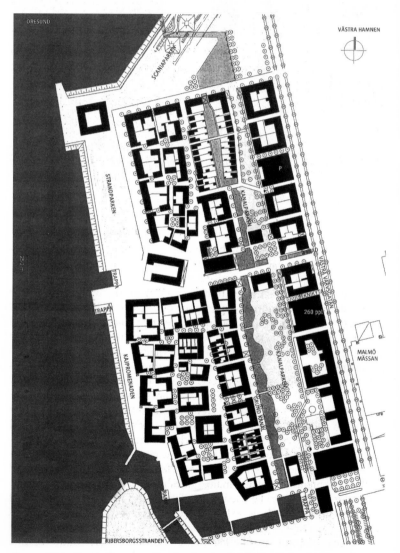

**Figure 15.1**   Vastra Hamnen site plan for the Exhibition Bo01, 2001.

**Figure 15.2** Solar collectors operated by Sydcraft a district energy supplier on the Tegelborden block on the Sundspromenaden. Architect Mansson Dahlback. Photograph Christopher John Hancock.

An important component of the development is the inclusion of non-residential ground floor space for small businesses with access to the first floor to permit living above the premises.

There is a highly disciplined transport policy for the site. Streets are car free and parking is limited to one space per dwelling. However, the real innovation is the provision of a pool of electric vehicles charged by wind power to enable the residents to reach the city centre. A neighbourhood garage provides natural gas/biogas for alternative fuel cars.

Surprisingly there is no facility for harvesting rainwater which is directed via the canal to the sea. Wastewater goes to the city's main treatment plant. However, there is a sophisticated system for the management of other kinds of waste which comprises an underground twin pipe vacuum tube collection network. Residents have access to twin terminals, one for food waste, the other for residual dry waste which is incinerated. Biogas and compost are obtained from the food waste. The city has constructed a reactor to convert organic waste into biogas and fertilizer. The biogas is returned to the apartments via the gas main. Nutrients and phosphorous are extracted from sewerage to be used as fertilizer with the residue used as fuel for the incinerator. It is estimated that reclaiming waste generates 290 kW h/year of energy for every resident.

The final innovation is the fact that all households are connected to a broadband communication network which provides information on a wide range of topics. This includes the ability to monitor the use of energy and water and to exploit an environmental advice channel as well as such essential data as the time the next bus will arrive at the nearest bus stop.

The overall impact of Vastra Hamnen is of a project that has, with its variety of architects, achieved a reconciliation between market forces and environmental priorities.

The masterplan has maximized the contrast between the expansive views to the sea and intimate green spaces encompassed by the apartments. A further asset is the parkland adjacent to the canal which all adds up to an urban complex which capitalizes on the spectacular location of the site. The dialectic between public and private space, between hard and soft landscape, between introvert and extravert space makes this a stimulating example of twenty-first century urban design. The final seal on the scheme will be the residential tower by Santiago Calatrava called the 'Turning Torso' which may sound more poetic in Swedish. It is due to be completed in 2003. If there has to be a criticism it is that architectural individuality has priority over a consistent urban grain. But with an exhibition site that is to be expected. Altogether it is not a bad template for a 'city of the future'.

## Government training centre, Germany

Possibly the most ambitious example of building-integrated PV (BIPV) to date is at the heart of the Ruhr in Germany at Herne-Sodingen. The Mount Cenis Government Training Centre claims to be the world's most powerful solar electric plant and is a spectacular demonstration of the country's commitment to rehabilitate this former industrial region while also signalling the country's commitment to ecological development (see Fig. 15.3).

After the demise of heavy industry the Ruhr became a heavily polluted wasteland which prompted the government of North-Rhine Westphalia to embark on an extensive regeneration programme covering 800 km².

The building is a giant canopy encompassing a variety of buildings and providing them with the climate of the Mediterranean. At 168 m long and 16 m high the form and scale of the building has echoes of the huge manufacturing sheds of former times. A timber structural frame of rough hewn pine columns is a kind of reincarnation of the forests from which they originated.

The structure encloses two three-storey buildings either side of an internal street running the length of the building (see Fig. 15.4).

The concrete structure provides substantial thermal mass, balancing out both diurnal and seasonal temperature fluctuations. Landscaped spaces provide social areas which can be used all year in a climate akin to the Côte d'Azure. Sections of the façade can be opened in summer to provide cross-ventilation.

The building is designed to be self-sufficient in energy. The roof and façade incorporate 10,000 m² of PV cells integrated with glazed panels. Two types of solar module were employed: monocrystalline cells with a peak

**Figure 15.3**  Mount Cenis In-service Training Centre, Herne-Sodingen, Germany.

efficiency of 16% and lower density polycrystalline cells at 12.5%. These provide a peak output of 1 MW. Six hundred converters change the current from DC to AC to make it compatible with the grid. A 1.2 MW battery plant stores power from the PVs, balancing output fluctuations. The power generated greatly exceeds the needs of the building at 750,000 kWh per year. German policy on renewables makes exporting to the grid a profitable proposition.

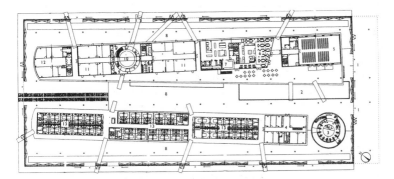

**Figure 15.4**  Mount Cenis ground floor plan.

This is not the only source of energy generation. The former mines in the area release more than 1 million m³ of methane which is used to provide both heat and power. Capturing the gas in this way results in a reduction of carbon dioxide emissions of 12,000 tonnes.

This complex is an outstanding example of an alliance between green technology and aesthetics. The architects, Jourda & Perraudin of Paris, designed the distribution of PV panels to reflect the arbitrary distribution of clouds by means of six different types of module with different densities creating subtle variations to the play of light within the interior. It all adds up to an enchanting environment of spaciousness, light and shade. At the same time it affords a graphic reminder that regenerated industrial landscapes do not have to be populated by featureless utilitarian sheds.

It is still the case that most PV arrays on buildings are installed for reasons that do not include cost effectiveness. However, that could change if the cost of the PVs is absorbed into the overall cost of a building refurbishment.

In many cases multi-storey commercial buildings are given a new facade at intervals of about every 15–20 years. Rather than dismantle the old curtain wall, it may well be cost effective to add a second external screen thereby creating a ventilation plenum. The next logical step is to incorporate PVs into the façade as panel elements. This should significantly improve the cost-benefit equation. In 1998 the British Columbia Institute of Technology Centre for Technology launched the Photovoltaic Energy Applied Research Lab (PEARL). One of its aims was to demonstrate that the cost of PVs could be reduced significantly by combining energy production with other functions of the building envelope. The outcome was a number of building integrated PV demonstration schemes, one of which was the Telus telecommunication company building in Vancouver.

The building was due for refurbishment and the option of providing an additional glazed rainscreen was adopted. The space between the two screens acts as a plenum for ventilation air. Ventilation driven by the stack effect was considered inadequate so 12 high-efficiency DC fans were installed. These are powered by an array of semi-transparent polycrystalline solar modules incorporated within the new curtain walls and delivering 2.5 kWp.

This is not ground-breaking green technology but it does point the way to much more ambitious exploitation of the potential to use the building façade as a power plant when refurbishment is being considered (see Fig. 15.5).

A problem which is becoming increasingly evident is that some of the claims for environmentally advanced designs have not been substantiated in the finished product, a situation brought to light largely through the efforts of the PROBE investigations. This is a project to investigate the post-occupancy performance of buildings aspiring to qualify as bioclimatic designs. The project is conducted by the *Building Services Journal*.

Exemplar buildings are often clear architectural statements of their green credentials. This is not an adverse criticism since such buildings advertise

**Figure 15.5** Telus Building, Vancouver. (Courtesy of *Renewable Energy World*.)

the emergence of a new architectural vocabulary. It is interesting therefore that the best performing building investigated by the PROBE team is an unassuming extension to a regional tax office in the Dutch city of Enschede (see Fig. 15.6). The building was part funded under the EU Energy Comfort 2000 project. The philosophy behind this scheme is that buildings should meet a range of comfort criteria, and that such an objective should have priority over financial constraints. The tax office is a prime example of a design by architect Ruurd Roorda which places occupant satisfaction at the top of the agenda.

The extension has five storeys with a wedge shaped atrium occupying the centre of the plan. Cellular offices 5 m deep occupy the north and south sides of the building. Access to the offices is gained from a gallery along the north side of the atrium with bridges serving the deeper plan south-side offices.

It is designed to be naturally ventilated with background ventilation provided by trickle ventilators. Rapid ventilation is provided by tilt and turn windows. Stale air leaves the offices through acoustically dampened ducts

**Figure 15.6**   Enschede Tax Office extension, The Netherlands.

running above suspended ceilings over corridors to the edge of the atrium. Exhaust air then rises in the atrium through stack effect to exit the building through six large chimneys. The natural ventilation system is backed up by four fans in the roof adjacent to the atrium clerestory windows on the north elevation. These are used on summer nights when there is little wind movement.

A central building management system (BMS) controls the heating, mechanical and night ventilation and external shading.

Considerable care has been taken to modulate the natural lighting to minimize glare and enable natural light to reach the inner limits of the cellular offices. Windows incorporate a 900 mm light shelf with a mirrored upper surface. These serve to reduce glare near the window and reflect light from the 3 m high white ceilings to the inner zone.

Solar gain through the south-facing façade is controlled by motorized external louvres. They are automatically activated by the BMS when the incident solar angle reaches a preset threshold. However, importantly, both the lowering of the louvres and their pitch can both be manually overridden. The occupants have manually controlled internal blinds shading the lower section of the window leaving the light shelf clear to perform its function.

One of the outstanding energy conservation characteristics of the building is its air tightness. Pressure testing by the UK Building Research Establishment was carried out in May 2001. The reference pressure is 50 pascals (Pa). The test measures the amount of air change per hour per square metre of façade. The result was 4.9 $m^3/h/m^2$ of façade. This is a result which reflects a design programme which demanded good air tightness construction from the outset. By comparison, a reference group of six offices including some designed to be airtight, produced a figure of over 15 m³/h/m² of envelope.

To offset the demand for grid electricity there is a roof mounted array of photovoltaics producing 8100 kWh/year. The electricity imported from the grid amounts to 34 kW h/m² which equates with the good practice benchmark. However, this includes high consumption for equipment in comparison with an exceptionally low consumption for building services.

What really marks this building as exceptional is the result of the user survey which is the ultimate test.

What stood out was the satisfaction at the degree of personal control that the building services afforded and the speed with which the building responded to optimize comfort. The shallow plan form, the cellular offices, thermal stability and good background ventilation all rated highly in the investigation. There was particular praise for the extent to which individuals could override control over such things as the external shading, automatic dimming and night-time ventilation. There was also satisfaction at the way artificial lighting and glare could be controlled.

An important element in success of this building is the way in which the operation of the services has been explained to the building users. A user guide is printed onto an A2 blotter for desk use. The systems are explained in words and pictures. Also there is constant access to facilities manager support. All this results in a rare level of symbiosis between a building and its occupants.

## Council offices, King's Lynn

Like the tax officials of Enschede, the Borough Council of King's Lynn in Norfolk were obliged to consider new accommodation and were committed to creating a building which was exemplary in both aesthetic and environmental terms. The Borough Council takes its obligations under Agenda 21 extremely seriously.

King's Lynn is a tight-knit town with buildings spanning from the twelfth to twenty-first centuries. The new offices occupy a corner site close to a Grade 1 listed church. Jeremy Stacey Architects were commissioned to produce a design which acknowledged the visual 'grain' of the town whilst offering an environmental performance which would place it amongst the leaders in ecological design (see Fig. 15.7).

The fabric of the building achieves standards well above regulations for thermal efficiency:

|  | U-values (W/m² K) |
|---|---|
| Roof | 0.13 |
| Walls | 0.20 |
| Ground floor | 0.16 |
| Windows triple glazed with integral venetian blinds | 1.7 |

**Figure 15.7**   Borough Council Offices, King's Lynn, Norfolk. (Courtesy of Ecotech.)

Careful detailing achieves an air infiltration rate of 5 m$^3$/h/m$^2$ of the building envelope at 50 Pa.

For ventilation the technology chosen was the Termodeck system in which ducts are incorporated into the concrete floor planks (see Chapter 3). One hundred per cent fresh air is mechanically supplied to each room with the corridors used as return air ducts. Condensing boilers provide heat for the air-handling system. This unit also ensures that 90% of the heat in exhaust air is recovered. In summer, night-time cooling of the fabric keeps the daytime temperature to within 3°C of the normal set control temperature for refrigeration-based systems. Exposed ceiling soffits provide the radiant cooling. All this means that there is virtually no maintenance burden associated with the ventilation, heating and cooling of the offices. The occupants have additional control over ventilation by being able to open windows.

Solar panels with electrical back-up provide the energy for the hot water system.

The running costs of the offices stand at about one quarter those for a fully air-conditioned equivalent which reinforces the axiom that green buildings really do pay.

This is an aesthetically, 'well mannered' building but it represents the level of commitment to ecological imperatives which must become universal if buildings are ever to shed their image as the key drivers of global warming through their associated carbon dioxide emissions.

## Cambridge USHER project

It seems appropriate to include in this sample of best practice a demonstration project which links buildings and transport with leading edge tech-

**Figure 15.8** PV Colonnade as conceived in principle by Whitby Bird.

nology. The University of Cambridge is developing a new science campus to the west of the city. It is associating with the Swedish city of Visby on the island of Gotland to create an integrated buildings and transport project in both countries.

The City Council in Cambridge has required as a condition of planning consent that a colonnade 350 m long and 10 m wide should be included in the masterplan (see Fig. 15.8).

One purpose of the colonnade is to provide a platform for electricity production which in turn would provide a zero emissions transport link with the centre of the city.

The roof of the colonnade will accommodate 3500 m$^2$ of cadmium telluride (CdTe) photovoltaic cells with a peak output of 300 kW and will generate over 260,000 kW h of DC current per year. The array at Visby will be 2500 m$^2$ generating 200 kWp. It will be integrated into a municipal building. The PVs at both sites will be dedicated to producing hydrogen to power fuel cell buses. An electrolyser will split water into hydrogen and oxygen, with the hydrogen stored at 200 bar pressure. The hydrogen will drive proton exchange membrane fuel cells (PEMFCs) as described in Chapter 7 (see Fig. 15.9).

In Cambridge the 30-seat fuel cell bus will operate between the Science Campus and the city centre. Its only emissions will be water vapour. In Visby the bus will transport people from the harbour to the main town via the old city. In summer, when the PVs will be at their most productive, the island receives over 500,000 tourists.

In Chapter 7 there was reference to a variation on this theme in which a fuel cell in a car would be plugged into a home or office to provide space heating and hot water for the 96% of the time the average car is stationary. The electricity would be sold to the grid. A recent report by a UK motoring organization predicts that all vehicles will be hydrogen powered by 2050.

These are small steps onto the threshold of the energy revolution which will inevitably occur in the first half of this century.

The progress towards this clean energy era could be hampered by a classic Catch-22 situation. Energy companies will not go to the expense of providing a hydrogen infrastructure until there is an adequate market for the product which, in turn, will not appear until there is a viable infrastructure. The only answer is for market development for fuel cells to take place by initially obtaining the hydrogen from reformed natural gas. The most urgent need is for the transport sector to embrace this technology. One solution would be for there to be a network of garages which reform natural gas on site and store at 200 bar. Already a number of forecourts are covered with PV cells. If these were dedicated to powering an electrolyser with backup from a natural gas reformer, this would enable the petrol companies to offer the hydrogen alternative and thus ease the transition to the hydrogen economy. Two or three such garages in major towns and

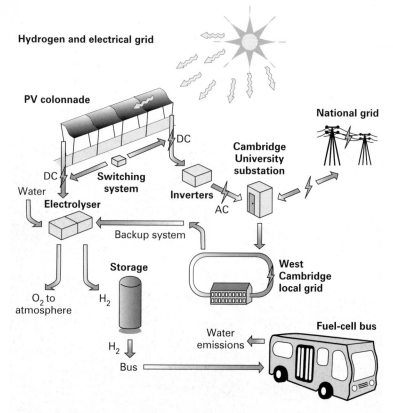

**Figure 15.9**  Outline of the project courtesy of Whitby Bird & Partners, consulting engineers to the scheme.

cities would not represent an intolerable investment cost for BP or Shell and would do wonders for their green credentials. At the same time it would give an impetus to vehicle manufacturers to accelerate production of fuel cell vehicles, currently scheduled to be on the market by 2005.

## Beddington Zero Energy Development (BedZED)

BedZED is not just another low-energy housing scheme, it is a prescription for a social revolution; a prototype of how we should live in the twenty-first century if we are to enjoy a sustainable future. This project was introduced at the foundations stage in *Architecture in a Climate of Change.*[1] The scheme now has its first residents and it is appropriate in this volume to consider the completed product (see Fig. 15.10).

It shares many of the objectives of the Malmo development and so makes an interesting comparison. The main difference is that there is a just one design team led by Bill Dunster Architects who is one of the UK's top evangelists for ecologically sustainable architecture.

To recapitulate, the Innovative Peabody Trust commissioned this development as an ultra-low energy mixed use scheme in the London Borough of Sutton. It consists of 82 homes with 271 habitable rooms, 2500 m$^2$ of space for offices, workspaces, studios, shops and community facilities including a nursery, organic shop and health centre, all constructed on the site of a former sewage works – the ultimate brownfield site. The housing comprises a mix of one- and two-bedroom flats, maisonettes and town houses.

**Figure 15.10**  Completed project west elevation.

Peabody was able to countenance the additional costs of the environmental provisions on the basis of the income from the offices as well as the homes. Though the Trust is extremely sympathetic to the aims of the scheme, it had to stack up financially.

In every respect this is an integrated and environmentally advanced project. It is a high density development along the line recommended by the Rogers Urban Task Force.

It realizes an overall density of 50 dwellings per hectare plus 120 workspaces per hectare. At such a density almost 3 million homes could be provided on brownfield sites with the additional benefit of workspaces for the occupants, radically cutting down on greenfield development and on the demand for travel. This density includes the provision of 4000 m$^2$ of green space including sports facilities. Excluding the sports ground and placing cars beneath the 'village square' the density could be raised to 105 homes and 200 workspaces per hectare.

Some dwellings have ground-level gardens while the roofs of the north-facing work spaces serve as gardens for the adjacent homes (see Fig. 15.11).

The energy efficiency of the construction matches anything in the UK or mainland Europe. External walls consist of concrete block inner leaf, 300 mm of rockwool insulation and an outer skin of brick adding up to a U-value of 0.11 W/m$^2$ K (see Fig. 15.12).

Roofs also contain 300 mm of insulation in this case styrofoam with a U-value of 0.10. Floors contain 300 mm of expanded polystyrene also having

**Figure 15.11** South elevation with work spaces at ground level and roof gardens serving dwellings opposite.

**Figure 15.12**  Masonry wall construction.

a U-value of 0.10. Windows are triple glazed with Low-E glass and argon filled. They are framed in timber and have a U-value of 1.20. These standards of insulation are a considerable improvement over those required by Part L of the 2002 Building Regulations in the UK. Masonry external and internal walls and concrete floors provide substantial thermal mass sustaining warmth in winter and preventing overheating in summer. In traditional construction up to 40% of warmth is lost through air leakage. In the case of BedZED great attention has been paid to maximizing air tightness which is designed to achieve two air changes per hour at 50 Pa.

One of its primary aims was to make the most of recycled materials and the main success in this respect was to obtain high grade steel from a demolished building as well as timber. The majority of all the materials were sourced within a 35-mile radius.

Materials containing volatile organic compounds (VOCs) have been avoided as part of the strategy to use low allergy materials.

Ventilation becomes an important issue as better levels of air tightness are achieved. In this case the design team opted for passive natural ventilation with heat recovery driven by roof cowls. A vane mounted on the cowls ensures that they rotate so that incoming air always faces upwind with exhaust air downwind. The heat recovery element captures up to 70% of the heat from the exhaust air.

The energy efficiency drive does not end there. South facing elevations capitalize on solar gain with windows and their frames accounting for nearly 100% of the wall area. Sun spaces embracing two floors on the south elevation add to the quality of the accommodation (see Figs 15.13 and 15.14).

According to the UK government's method of measuring the energy performance of buildings, the Standard Assessment Procedure for Energy Rating of Dwellings (1998) (SAP) BedZED achieves 150. Until the 2002 revision of the Regulations dwellings were required to achieve around SAP 75. It is predicted that space heating costs will be reduced by 90% against a SAP 75 building. Overall energy demand should be reduced by 60%.

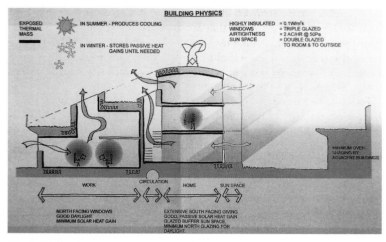

**Figure 15.13** Section showing the passive features. (Courtesy of ARUP and BRE.)

BedZED aims to reduce domestic water consumption by 33%. This is to be achieved by the use of water-saving toilets, dishwashers and washing machines. Toilets normally use 9 litres per flush; regulations now stipulate a 7.5 litre maximum. Here 3.5 litre dual flush toilets are provided producing

**Figure 15.14** South elevation with PVs integrated into the glazing.

an estimated saving of 55,000 litres per household per year. Taps are fitted with flow restrictors; showers that rely on gravity replace baths in single bedroom flats. As the scheme uses metered water it is expected that these measures will save a household £48 per year. On average, 18% of a household's water requirements will be met by rainwater stored in large tanks integrated into the foundations.

Foulwater is treated in a sewage treatment plant housed in a greenhouse. It is a biologically based system which uses nutrients in sewage sludge as food for plants. The output from the plant is of a standard equivalent to rainwater and therefore can supplement the stored rainwater to be used to flush toilets.

Household waste normally destined for landfill will be reduced by 80% compared with the average home.

## BedZED, the energy package

The principal energy source for the development is a combined heat and power unit that generates 130 kW of electric power. This is sufficient for the power needs of the scheme. The plant also meets its space heating and domestic hot water requirements via a district heating system served by insulated pipes. The CHP plant is reckoned to be of adequate output due to the high standard of insulation and air tightness and the fact that the peaks and troughs of seasonal and diurnal temperature are flattened by the high thermal mass of the houses.

A combustion engine generates the heat and power producing 350,000 kWh of electricity per year. It is fuelled by a mixture of hydrogen, carbon monoxide and methane produced by the on-sight gasification of wood chips which are the waste product from nearby managed woodlands. The waste would otherwise go to landfill. The plant requires 1100 tonnes per year which translates to two lorry loads per week. In the future rapid rotation willow coppicing from the adjacent ecology park will supplement the supply of woodland waste. Across London 51,000 tonnes of tree surgery waste is available for gasification. It is worth restating that this is virtually a carbon neutral route to energy since carbon taken up in growth is returned to the atmosphere. Excess electricity is sold to the grid whilst any shortfall in demand is met by the grid's green tariff electricity. It is predicted that the scheme will be a net exporter to the grid (see Chapter 8 and Fig. 15.15).

There is a further chapter to the energy story. Figure 15.16 illustrates the inclusion of PVs in the south glazed elevations of the scheme. They are also sited on southerly facing roofs. Their purpose is to provide a battery charging facility for electric vehicles. How the decision was made to dedicate the PVs to this role is worth recording.

Originally the idea was to use PVs to provide for the electricity needs of the buildings. Evacuated tube solar collectors would provide the heating. It turned out that this arrangement would involve a 70-year payback

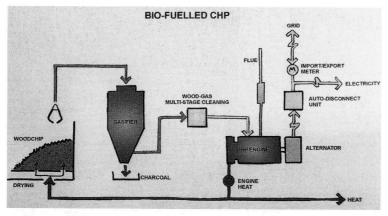

**Figure 15.15**   Wood chip gasification plant within the development. (Courtesy of ARUP and BRE.)

timescale. If the electricity were to be used to displace the use of fossil fuels in vehicles, taking into account their high taxation burden, the payback time would be about 13 years. So, it was calculated that 777 m$^2$ of high efficiency monocrystalline PVs would provide a peak output of 109 kW, sufficient for the energy needs of 40 light electric vehicles covering 8500 km per year. It has to be remembered that, in a project like BedZED, the energy used by a conventional car could greatly exceed that used in the dwelling. As a yardstick, a family car travelling 12,000 miles (19,000 km) per year produces almost as much carbon as a family of four living in a typical modern home.

The aim is that the 40 vehicles would provide a pool of cars to be hired by the hour by residents and commercial tenants. Other car pool schemes have indicated that hiring a pool car to cover up to 13,000 km a year could save around £1500 in motoring costs. And that is without factoring in the potential avoided cost of pollution. With congestion charges due to be levied on vehicles using streets in major cities, the exemption of electric vehicles will provide an even greater incentive to adopt this technology.

The co-developers Peabody and Bioregional agreed as part of the terms of the planning consent to enter into a Green Travel Plan which meant a commitment to minimize the residents' environmental impact from travel. On-site work and recreational facilities together with the electric vehicle pool of 'Zedcars' would more than satisfy that commitment.

Figure 15.16 produced by Arup summarizes the ecological inventory of the project .

This development has come about because the right people were able to come together in the right place at the right time. The idea came from Bioregional Development Group, an environmental organization based in Sutton who secured Peabody as the developer. Peabody is one of the most

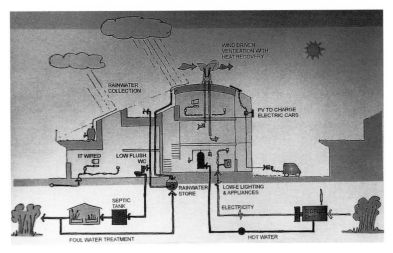

**Figure 15.16** The ecological inventory of BedZED. (Courtesy of ARUP and BRE.)

enlightened housing associations in Britain. Bill Dunster was engaged on the strength of Hope House which he designed as an ecologically sound living/working environment and which served as a prototype for BedZED. Chris Twinn of Ove Arup & Partners worked with Bill Dunster when the latter was with Michael Hopkins & Partners so he was a natural choice as adviser on the physics and services of BedZED. The project happened due to a fortuitous conjunction of people committed to the principles of sustainable development. In future, developments of this nature must not rely on the chance collision of the brightest stars in the environmental firmament.[2]

## 'Skyzed'

Tower blocks are usually regarded as the antithesis of green building. Bill Dunster Architects have tackled this perception head-on with the concept design for a zero energy tower. The argument is that urban densities will have to increase which will make some high-rise development inevitable, therefore the task is to exploit their height and floor plate to make them net sources of power. The tower could form the focal point of a larger low rise housing complex on the lines of BedZED and could rise to 35 storeys.

The tower consists of four lobes or 'petals' which direct the wind into a central void containing wind turbines. Wind velocity tests indicate that air flow at the core of the building would be multiplied four-fold by the configuration of the petal plan. This would be sufficient to power several vertical axis turbines which would be almost silent. At the same time the floor plates are designed to provide maximum views whilst optimizing daylight (see Fig. 15.17).

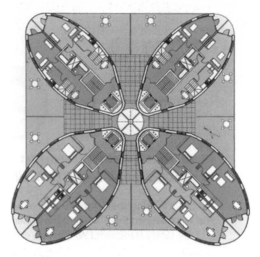

**Figure 15.17**   Skyzed accommodation lobes which gave rise to the term 'flower tower'.

On every fourth floor there are triple-glazed lobbies linking the petals and providing platforms for viewing the turbines. Additional electricity is provided by PVs on the south-facing façade and south-sloping roofs. According to engineers Whitby Bird the combination of low and high rise housing would be self-sufficient in electricity (see Fig. 15.17).

To complete its sustainability credentials all grey and black water would be recycled via reed beds located in the shadow of the tower. Much of the construction would employ reclaimed materials: ground granulated blast-furnace slag (ggbs) would be a concrete aggregate while reclaimed timber would provide stressed-skin panels.

The commercial viability of the project would be enhanced by the inclusion of work and community spaces on the ground floor. The high density of 115 homes per hectare is the factor which does most for the marketability of the project. That should keep the accountants happy. What would keep the residents happy is the possibility of living and working within the locality of the site whilst enjoying the benefits of ultra-low energy construction.

The conclusion to be drawn from these case studies is that sustainable design is a holistic activity and demands an integrated approach. Reducing the demand for energy and generating clean energy are two sides of the same coin. Examples have been cited where buildings and transport are organically linked with building integrated renewables providing power for electric cars. BedZed and to some extent Malmo are signposts to new and much more sustainable and agreeable patterns of life. This book has

**Figure 15.18**   SkyZed tower and in context.

been an attempt to illustrate how the link between buildings and renewable technologies can form a major part of the green revolution which must happen if there is to be any chance of stabilizing atmospheric carbon dioxide at a level which leaves the planet tolerably habitable.

## Notes

1.  Smith PF. *Architecture in a Climate of Change*, pp. 76–78. Oxford: Architectural Press, 2001.
2.  For a more detailed description of this project, refer to 'General Information Report 89, BedZED – Beddington Zero Energy Development, Sutton, published by BRECSU at BRE (brecsuenq@bre.co.uk).

# 16  Sustainability on a knife edge

Up to now most of the book has focused on the detail across a range of renewable energy technologies. As a conclusion I should like to place the drive for renewable energy in its wider context. It is time to confront the dilemma inherent in all renewable sources of energy and that is that they have to compete with abundant, cheap fossil fuels. The IPCC Third Assessment Report (TAR) states that 'there are abundant fossil fuel reserves that will not limit carbon emissions during the 21st century'. (Report from Working Group III.) It goes on to say that 'At least up to 2020, energy supply and conversion will remain dominated by relatively cheap and abundant fossil fuels'. In this it agrees with the industry forecasters like Professor Morris Adelman of MIT: 'For the next 25–50 years, the oil available to the market is, for all intents and purposes, infinite' (Economist Energy Survey 2001). We now have the added anxiety over the plans to tap untold reserves of underground coal by igniting it and drawing off methane. It is called underground coal gasification (UGC). The verdict of *New Scientist* on this development is: 'Whatever the local, short term benefits of adopting UGC, in the long run liberating even a fraction of the carbon stored in the world's subterranean coal reserves could create one hell of an environmental nightmare' (Fred Pearce, 1 June 2002).

In the stark analysis of current accountancy procedures renewable sources of energy are not cost effective. They *are* cost effective wherever it has been uneconomic to provide grid electricity or where that supply is expensive or unreliable. That certainly includes the 2 billion inhabitants of the planet who have no access to electricity. Renewable energy must be a major component of a strategy that aims at a sustainable future for the planet.

For the developed countries there has to be a motivational force that overrides the blinkered vision of neo-classical economics. Everything considered so far has to be placed in the context of the macro-economic and geophysical prospects for the next few decades because the planet is changing at a pace and on a scale greater than at any time since the big bang. The three main drivers of change are:

- globalization
- population
- climate change

all of which are the result of human activity and which all have serious implications for the future security and health of the planet.

## Globalization

The first thing to be said is that globalization is an irreversible fact just as information technology cannot be dis-invented. However, in its present manifestation it is bipolarizing the affluent and the poor.

A UN Human Development Report states:

> *The greatest benefits of globalisation have been garnered by a fortunate few ...*
> *If present trends continue, economic disparities between industrial and developing nations will move from inequitable to inhuman.*[1]

There are two elements to this phenomenon. The first concerns the trade in money. National economies are now at the mercy of computerized trading that can move trillions of dollars almost at the speed of light. Massive flows of money can be an almost instantaneous response to a market event on a scale which is usually out of all proportion to the market importance of that event. It can throw whole regions into chaos as it did in 1998 when the Asian stock market lost $2 trillion. Economies ground to a halt; there was a drastic fall in the demand for raw materials and services; in Russia the rouble collapsed in response to a fall in the sale of oil. Years of growth were wiped out overnight and millions were thrown out of work. All this in response to the virtual reality of the stock market.

The second element is the rise of transnational corporations and their dominance of the World Trade Organization (WTO). That they are now able to manipulate national governments is illustrated by the fact that 51 of the world's 100 biggest economies are transnationals. General Motors' annual sales are greater than the GNP of Norway; Ford outstrips the GNP of Poland and the most predatory of them all, WalMart, exceeds the GNP of Saudi Arabia, Greece, Portugal and Venezuela. Overall, the richest 20% of the planet own 86% of its wealth. Within the most free market of all, the US, nearly 40% of national wealth is owned by 1% of the population. This contrasts with 20% in the 1970s.

National governments are yielding more and more to transnationals out of fear that they can easily move to places with more amenable jurisdictions such as lax labour laws and attractive tax regimes. The ultimate expression of this is the WTO which is the instrument of economic control exercised by the developed nations. As *The Guardian* put it earlier this year, the WTO has become the enforcer, not of free trade, but coercive trade ...

punishing states which try to defend their people'. Nothing must stand in the way of free trade, including environmental and health considerations.

A UN report of July 2001 states that 'The global free market doesn't work. However much it benefits corporations and consumers in rich countries, for most people it is a dismal failure. It's done nothing to lift the hideous burden of disease, poverty and ignorance from the world's poorest nations.'

It wasn't always like this. The forerunner of the WTO was GATT, the General Agreement on Tariffs and Trade created in 1947. Its aim was to remove unfair trade barriers and enable poor countries to trade on equal terms with the rich. However, a succession of corporate lawyers changed its stance, inserting clauses that facilitated unconditional corporate rule. In 1995 GATT was replaced by the WTO by which time it had become the means by which corporations could force governments to open their borders to every possible kind of exploitation. Nothing would be allowed to stand in the way of free trade, certainly not environmental, health, humanitarian, or animal rights considerations. So, the UK cannot refuse to accept asbestos from Canada. Europe did refuse to accept American beef injected with six hormones, one of which is thought possibly to be a cause of cancer in children. As a penalty the WTO allowed the US to impose $160 million worth of sanctions against the European Union. It has been alleged that a large manufacturer is invoking WTO rules to force genetically modified (GM) foods on unwilling populations. The European Union Environment Commissioner has expressed fears that the Union will be sued if it does not allow the sale of new GM foods.

At the same time, one of the founding principles of GATT is still being abused, namely the removal of tariffs. Europe continues to levy massive tariffs on cotton goods from India. Rich countries continue to destroy the livelihoods of farmers in the south by saturating their markets with subsidized grain. The WTO has gone even further down the route of protectionism by granting multinational companies exclusive ownership of plant varieties.

The other powerful instrument of economic coercion is the International Monetary Fund (IMF). This fund was set up after the second world war to provide emergency short-term loans to Western countries with balance of payments problems. Since then its focus has shifted to poor countries. In 1999 the G7 countries offered debt relief of $100 billion which was nearly half the outstanding debt. But there are strings attached. The IMF now sees its role as the enforcer of economic so-called reforms. To qualify for debt relief a country must spend 6 years on an IMF 'structural adjustment programme'. This usually means it must increase interest rates, cut its budget deficit and devalue its currency. It may also mean the country must open its borders to foreign goods, privatize state-owned enterprises and deregulate their financial and banking sectors; the standard *laissez-faire* formula. One of the most onerous conditions is that a country must limit its production capacity to only one or two exports, making it highly vulnerable to market fluctuations or climatic disasters.

The verdict of the Overseas Development Institute is that structural adjustment programmes merely succeed in widening existing inequalities, increasing the burden which falls on the urban poor.

The position now is that 50 countries are described as 'hyper-indebted'. A measure of the stress experienced by poor countries is to relate debt to GNP. In Africa the average ratio of debt to GNP is 123%. In other words, for every $100 of GNP there is $123 of outstanding debt. Each week sub-Saharan African countries pay $250 million in debt repayments to the richest countries. There is no chance of such countries dancing to the IMF's tune for debt relief.

The situation regarding globalization was recently summed up by billionaire financier George Soros: 'I believe that the global capitalist system in its present form is a distortion of what ought to be a global open society'.[2]

What has all this to do with renewable energy? One of the main routes to empowerment for the exploited and impoverished populations of the earth is through access to energy. It is worth repeating that one-third of the world's population has no access to electricity. They will never be connected to a grid, therefore renewable technologies are the only answer. Examples have been cited of how micro-hydro has transformed remote village life. A massive programme of capital and technology transfer will be required not just to deal with inequalities now, but to alleviate the inevitable impacts of future climate change which will hit hardest at developing countries.

At a most basic level access to electricity facilitates refrigeration of food and storing of medicines, boiling of drinking water, etc. But one of the most important benefits is the access to information and learning through information technology. Just one example will have to suffice. A group of villages on the east coast of India near Chennai (previously known as Madras) have formed a network to share computer information. A central receiving station relays information to the villages, each of which has two or three computers. Fishing villages get up to date weather reports, even to the expected wave height; they find the going market price for fish, rice and other products in local markets; they access government information on how to tackle crop disease; they can call a doctor and many other facilities which have transformed their lives. The centre also offers computer courses for 50 rupees a month (roughly $1). Women in the villages have been particularly quick to exploit this facility. Access to the Internet is already changing people's lives in parts of India and the key is the availability of electricity.

Information technology is one of the most promising means of narrowing the gap between rich and poor. As Ian Angell (Head of the Department of Information Systems, London School of Economics) puts it:

*People with computer skills are likely to end up winners. Those without are likely to emerge as losers ... The information age will be kindest to those who adapt.*

Given the opportunity, people in the developing world adapt rapidly to information technology, helping them to take the first steps in avoiding the kind of exploitation to which globalization in its present form has subjected them. Following the failure of the June 2002 Bali conference to set the agenda for the August Earth Summit at Johannesburg, *The Guardian* concluded: 'many observers now believe the best result possible for Johannesburg would be a new focus on Africa and a new series of government initiatives, backed by industry, to introduce new technologies such as solar power and computers to poor countries'.

## The population time bomb

The second driver for change is the anticipated population growth. On 12 October 1999 world population passed the 6 billion mark. It is increasing by 1.4 times per year. That may not seem much but in fact represents exponential growth. The pattern of population expansion has been described as bacterial rather than primate.

It is true that the rate of reproduction is falling; in 1960 the world average for a woman was 4.3 children; by 2000 it had dropped to 2.6. To achieve stability this needs to fall to 2.1. The 0.1 accounts for infant mortality. Even slightly over the 2.1 means that the growth remains exponential.

Ultimately for a variety of reasons world population will peak. The UN Department of Economic and Social Affairs estimates that it could reach 14.4 billion by 2050 but is more likely to peak at 10 billion. In theory the world can produce enough grain to feed 10 billion, provided they are east Indians who eat primarily grains and very little meat. The same amount of grain would support only 2.5 billion Americans who convert much of their grain to foodstock for animals to meet their mountainous appetite for steaks.

The problem is that almost all this estimated population growth will occur in developing countries in which the drive towards higher per capita consumption will be relentless, especially in China.

China may well serve to give a foretaste of the future. By 2000 it had reached 1.2 billion population; by 2030 at this rate it will reach 1.6 billion. The crucial factor is that the great bulk of this population is concentrated in the great valleys of the Yangtze and Yellow Rivers and their tributaries, an area about the size of the USA. China is on the verge of consuming more than it can produce. By 2025 it will be importing 175 million tonnes of grain per year and 200 million tonnes by 2030 which equals present total world exports (US National Intelligence Council).

China relies heavily on aquifers and the great rivers for irrigation purposes. Four-fifths of the available water is from the Yangtze in the south. In the north there are already severe shortages. For example, the water table under Beijing fell 37 m between 1965 and 1995. Per capita water consumption is rising with economic growth. By 2030 it is expected that household demand will have increased fourfold to 234 billion tonnes and industrial demand five times to 269 billion tonnes. Yet already 300 of its 617 cities are experiencing severe water stress which is having an impact on the price of water to the detriment of agriculture. The reason is this: 1000 tonnes of fresh water yields 1 tonne of wheat worth $200. The same amount used by industry yields a value of $14,000. The rapid industrialization of China is exacerbating the problem by the day and widening the divide between the poor and the affluent. Almost certainly China will drive up the world price of grain with dire consequences for other developing countries.

China represents the critical path for the future. How it solves its problems may give a lead to the rest of the world.

The inescapable fact is that the earth is finite and becoming increasingly brittle. There are ever-widening inequalities between industrialized and developing nations. Take the case of the ecological footprint, i.e. the area of land needed to meet the consumption of a single person. In the developing nations it is 1 hectare (2.5 acres) per person; in the US it is 9.4 hectares or 24 acres. The world average is 2.1 hectares or 5.2 acres. It would take four more planets the size of earth to enable the whole population to enjoy American levels of consumption.

Humans have become a geophysical force, perhaps irreversibly changing the biosphere to its detriment, living off unsustainable crop yields, drying out aquifers, erasing whole ecosystems.

## Climate change

The third factor which is stressing the planet is global warming and its climatic consequences.

The uncomfortable truth is that if we achieved a 90% cut in anthropogenic carbon dioxide emissions now it would do little to halt the march of climate change for the first half of the century. The momentum already built up in the system will sustain global warming for several decades to come. This forces us to acknowledge two imperatives:

- By means of technology and capital transfer from the industrialized nations, to do everything possible to soften the impact of climate change on the most vulnerable populations.
- To shift as rapidly as possible from reliance on fossil fuels to ensure that the final ceiling on atmospheric carbon dioxide is at a level to which ecosystems can adapt, at the same time avoiding the doomsday scenario of runaway global warming due to unstoppable positive feedback.

## The probable impacts

As John Houghton pointed out in the first chapter, sea levels are bound to rise exacerbated by storm surges which means that some of the most heavily populated coastal regions will be inundated. Inevitably this will mean massive movement of inhabitants; perhaps millions migrating across continents. Contingency plans should already be being formulated to accommodate the displaced populations. The problem is compounded by the fact that coastal plains are usually the most fertile agricultural regions.

On the 19 March 2002 it was reported that a huge portion of the Larson B ice shelf 3250 km$^2$ in area had broken loose from the Antarctic peninsula. The average temperature in this part of Antarctica has risen 2.5°C in 50 years which is five times the average rate of global warming. The importance of the ice shelves is that they buttress the land based ice. The ultimate scenario is that the ice shelves will disappear allowing land based ice to disintegrate and melt. This would produce a 5 m rise in sea level. Many of the world's major cities lie below this contour. The effect particularly on developing countries can barely be imagined.

Crop growing belts will shift, often across national boundaries, leading to cross-border tension as populations follow the crops. Animals and insects will move habitat in response to rapid climate change. Trees on the other hand have no such mobility raising the prospect of massive die-back of forests.

Access to water is predicted to be the most likely source of conflict between nations in this century. The case of China has been noted.

Glaciers are melting at an unprecedented rate. Initially this leads to floods. More dangerous still is the swelling of meltwater lakes in which the waters are retained by the debris deposited by glaciers at the end of their travel. These are unstable and some have already collapsed with dreadful results. The prediction is that some of the largest of these will give way within 5–10 years, leading to massive flooding of river valleys and catastrophic loss of life.

When all the glaciers have melted this too will have dire consequences for populations reliant for their existence on the great rivers for irrigation like the Ganges, Yangtze and Yellow rivers all fed by meltwater. It is estimated that all the glaciers in the central and eastern Himalayas will have disappeared by 2035.

Of all the pathways towards an *unsustainable* planet global warming is the superhighway.

The IPCC is noted for understating things yet it concludes:

> *Projected climate changes during the 21st century have the potential to lead to future large scale and possibly irreversible changes in Earth systems resulting in impacts at continental and global scales.*

In a book about renewable energy it may seem to have been a digression to switch to global problems. In a situation of abundant, cheap fossil-based energy it is necessary to draw in outline a picture of life on this planet if we continue to adhere to 'business as usual' and fail to invest in its future security. Motivation other than raw market forces is needed to make the transition to the fast track development and installation of renewable technologies in order to halt the rise in the accumulation of atmospheric carbon. Currently atmospheric concentrations of carbon dioxide at 350 parts per million by volume (ppmv) are at their highest for 420,000 years and probably 20 million years. The same can be said for methane which has increased 151% since 1750 due to human activity. The TAR has expanded on its original scenarios with its Special Report on Emission Scenarios (SRES). What it amounts to is the prediction that, by 2100, the level of atmospheric carbon dioxide will be between 540 and 970 ppmv. It should be remembered that the pre-industrial level was 280 ppmv. The business-as-usual ceiling is said to be 1260 ppmv, that is 350% higher than in 1750.

If we are already seeing significant climate changes, as indicated by the report, at 350 ppm concentration, the effect of 970 ppm is unimaginable, yet that is where we are heading at present.

The IPCC report slightly raises its temperature rise predictions over 1995. Now it peaks at a possible 5.8°C by 2100. But what really should set alarm bells ringing is this statement: 'all land areas will warm more rapidly than the global average, particularly those in the northern high latitudes in the cold season'. It adds that in certain parts the overland warming could be more than 40% higher than the global mean. We're talking of around 8.5°C probably in central southern Europe.

Even more disconcerting is the IPCC's conclusion that, even if we succeed in stabilizing atmospheric carbon dioxide, about 25% of the increase in concentration will persist in the atmosphere for several centuries and also temperatures will continue to rise over the same period. Sea level is also expected to continue to rise for centuries to come due to thermal expansion because of the long timescale on which the oceans adjust to climate change.

Ice sheets will continue to melt and contribute to sea level rise for hundreds of years after stabilization. The Greenland ice sheet alone would cause a 7 m rise and the Antarctic ice a 5 m rise in the long term.

In May 2002 the UN Environment Programme issues a 'Global Environment Outlook to 2032'. It is summed up in a stark choice. Either we stay with a 'market first' approach in which case carbon emissions will rise from the current 6.5 billion tonnes a year to 16 billion by 2032 with incalculable consequences, or we shift to 'sustainability first' capitalizing on renewable resources especially energy to stabilize carbon emissions and 'energize' the developing world.

The compelling argument for rapidly switching to low to zero carbon technologies is that the future of the planet could be determined by our actions within the next two decades.

To round things off we have to ask the question, why, in the face of such compelling and authoritative evidence are democratic governments and many of their electorate so half-hearted in their response to the challenge of climate change and its threat to future generations?

One possible answer is that there is a mood of fatalism about the geophysical forces that we are unleashing. Changing the direction of the supertanker earth is such a formidable prospect that it is easier to go into denial or believe the sceptics like Bjørn Lomborg. But maybe the real problem lies with human nature itself, or, more precisely, the human brain. Edward Wilson considers that evolutionary pressures gave high priority to achieving short-term benefits, that is, benefits for the immediate family or tribe. This attitude is hard-wired; a remnant of our paleolithic heritage. For hundreds of millennia those who strove for short-term gains for themselves and their immediate kin lived longer and left more offspring. This short-term horizon attitude is at the centre of the environmental problem. And short-termism isn't just a pathology of governments; it is inherent in the species. Unless we break its grip on the collective mind of humanity it is difficult to view the future with any measure of optimism. We have to get it across that if we take action *now* within the framework of long-term goals we should secure a somewhat altered planet for future generations. The alternative is to slide myopically into the abyss.

## Notes

1. *New Scientist*, p. 31, 27 April 2002.
2. *New Scientist*, p. 38,  27 April 2002.

# Index